6.95

S0-FQO-377

Anne Dare

Clockwatchers' Cookbook

Hamlyn
London · New York
Sydney · Toronto

Contents

Published by
The Hamlyn Publishing
Group Limited
London · New York · Sydney · Toronto
Hamlyn House, Feltham,
Middlesex, England
© Copyright 1973
Birds Eye Foods Limited
ISBN 0 600 31721 8
Printed in Spain by
Mateu Cromo, Madrid

Photographs specially taken by
Don Last

Dishes used in the photography
kindly loaned by Harvey Nichols &
Company Limited, Knightsbridge,
London, S.W.1

Stoneware jar, on page 20, from
David Mellor (Ironmonger), Sloane
Square, London, S.W.1

*Back cover picture shows a chicken
casserole with spring vegetables.*

Acknowledgements

**With grateful thanks to the
staff of the Birds Eye Kitchens,
both past and present, without
whose hard work this book
would never have been written—
and to my secretary who
patiently sorted it all out.**

Introduction

SELF-WINDING SUGGESTIONS

The key that winds the successful clockwatcher is planning.

There is nothing more time-wasting than being thoroughly disorganised. Have you noticed that many of the people who complain that they 'have not got time' usually live in what could be called perpetual chaos?

Since you're reading this book, you must be interested in saving yourself time in the kitchen and spending the time you've saved on other things which you enjoy more. So you're probably a planner anyway. If you are not, this book alone cannot even begin to help you!

Planning for cooking starts long before you open the first packet or write the first shopping list. It begins with the kitchen itself. Have you got all the labour-saving devices you deserve and can afford? There are some gadgets which save time and others which waste it.

CLOCKWATCHERS' KITCHEN

Few of us have the opportunity to design a kitchen exactly as we'd like it. Even if we have, doors and windows are often in the wrong places or the whole area is much too small to allow the kitchen of our dreams.

Thus the chance to plan the siting of cupboards, drawers and electrical appliances can be a challenge. To some people, it may be a bit unnerving. The best way to start is to imagine yourself doing as many of your routine tasks as you can think of, without moving your feet more than absolutely necessary. That way, you're bound to plan a kitchen that requires minimal effort.

Even if you can't plan your dream kitchen, there are usually improvements to be made to the one you already have. And some improvements can be made at little or no cost.

Do you keep your saucepans next to the cooker, your washing machine adjacent to the sink?

Is your main working area between the cooker and the sink, and are your cooking utensils handy when you prepare food?

Is the place where you stand most often, the most pleasant part of the kitchen?

Do you keep your coffee, sugar, cup and saucer near the kettle, or do you have to walk half a mile to make yourself a 'cuppa'?

These are small points, but they all add up to help the clockwatcher.

Auto-timed, self-cleaning ovens are the ultimate in time-saving equipment and the new, easy-clean oven finishes are a help too.

The development of refrigerators with larger frozen food compartments, which will store commercially frozen food for up to three months, are also invaluable to the clockwatcher, for they mean that she can store a large enough range of frozen food to cover any emergency or suit any household situation. The whole spectrum of convenience foods on the market today has altered our way of living. In some cases, we have come to accept their value to such an extent that they have become an integral part of our life. Few people can remember the days before canned food, and most people take pre-washed, dried, frozen and pre-packed foods entirely for granted.

The clockwatching housewife can happily make use of these for all types of occasions. She can spend more time enjoying her family, her guests or her job because she saves on food preparation and cooking time. And many convenience foods even reduce the amount of washing-up afterwards. With a vast and varied choice before her, she can use convenience foods widely, selecting perishable ingredients to enhance flavours, balance nutrition and provide added variety.

Life is better still if you have a home freezer. This is the ultimate in clock-watching. Shopping excursions are reduced to a minimum and you can even have bulk deliveries to your door. You can freeze your own cooked dishes and arrange cooking sessions only when you're in the mood. Dinner parties can be cooked far in advance, and so can meals for the school holidays, for weekends and packed lunches. In fact, they can all be prepared when YOU feel like it.

With a freezer too, you can also store sliced bread, quantities of fresh breadcrumbs, grated cheese, and rubbed-in fat and flour—ready to have sugar added for a crumble or water for pastry. In fact a freezer opens up a whole new aspect of cooking, and with it, a whole new way of life.

CLOCKWATCHERS' GADGETS

As well as the larger pieces of kitchen equipment, small items can also save you time. Mixers, liquidisers, percolators, and toasters all work while you do something else. There are many others, too. If you haven't any of the following, you're missing out on valuable time-savers—

rotary-grater
egg slicer
auto-chop
garlic press
wall can-opener or an electric one
onion-slicing fork
spiral hand whisk—very useful for
  omelettes
plastic spatula—invaluable for
  efficient scraping of bowls
kitchen scissors

flameproof casseroles—the type
  which can be used on top of the
  stove as well as in the oven, and
  then used at table
very sharp knives—a set of really
  good French ones is an
  investment you'll never regret
kitchen paper
foil—yards and yards of it
skewers—for an infinite number
  of tasks

There are many other gadgets, but *these* the good clockwatcher should never be without.

CLOCKWATCHERS' STORE CUPBOARD

If your kitchen is well organised already, then the store cupboard is the next item to plan. Most new houses have no walk-in larder and many people regret this. But with more temperature-controlled storage, which ideally should be sited in the kitchen, our need for other forms of storage will diminish. The efficient clockwatcher will have a wide variety of stores, reflecting her own and her family's preferences and needs.

EARLY BIRD COOKERY

Maybe you're the sort of person who can't stand the thought of any sort of breakfast. In that case, skip this chapter!

But if you would collapse halfway through the morning unless you ate a three-course meal, then this section is for you.

Normally, perhaps, you just snatch a cup of coffee in between feeding your husband and children and getting them out of the house on time. But there are times when breakfast is a more leisurely affair. Here are some recipes to break the routine, to enjoy even when you're in a hurry. And there are some to prepare at your leisure.

BREAKFASTS IN A TICK

Egg Flip

Cooking time: nil
Dish: 4 glasses
Serves: 4

6¼ fl. oz. can frozen concentrated orange juice, thawed   4 eggs

Dilute the orange juice according to pack instructions. Beat the eggs and then strain into the juice. Serve.

Handy hint: for two servings, reduce amount of juice and allow one egg each—mixing just before serving.

Florida Prunes

Cooking time: 10 minutes
Dish: shallow dish
Serves: 1

6—8 prunes, soaked overnight

¼ pint diluted frozen
   concentrated orange
   juice   } mix together
½ teaspoon clear honey

Put the prunes and water in a saucepan, bring slowly to the boil and simmer for 5 minutes. Drain and add prunes to the orange juice. Serve while prunes are still warm.

Handy hint: vitamin C in orange juice is well retained if not heated.

Beefburger Busters

Cooking time: 7 minutes
Dish: individual plates
Serves: 4

4 bread baps
1 large onion, sliced
cooking oil

4 home-made hamburgers *or*
   8 oz. frozen beefburgers
tomato sauce

Lightly toast the baps. Brush onion rings liberally with oil. Grill the beefburgers and the onion rings at the same time. Place beefburgers in the baps and fill with onion and tomato sauce. Serve hot.

Handy hint: grill beefburgers gently, to keep the round shape.

Orange/Chocolate Fancy

Cooking time: 5–10 minutes
Time to chill
Makes: 2¼ pints

6¼ fl. oz. can frozen concentrated orange juice, thawed
3 cans water

4 level tablespoons drinking chocolate
1 pint milk, chilled
whipped cream

Mix the orange juice with 2 cans of water and keep chilled. Blend the drinking chocolate with the remaining can of water in a pan, and bring to the boil, stirring. Cool. Pour on to the orange juice and mix well, then chill. Just before serving, stir in the milk. Serve in glasses topped with a teaspoonful of whipped cream.

Handy hint: if the orange and chocolate mixture is not all required at once, keep separate until serving.

Muesli

Cooking time: nil
Dish: shallow dish
Serves: 4

8 rounded tablespoons porridge oats
juice of 3 medium oranges
2 teaspoons honey
2 tablespoons 'top of milk'
1 apple, chopped

2 oz. grapes, pips removed
1 banana, skinned and sliced
1 orange, peeled and sliced
2 cartons natural yoghourt
1 oz. nuts, chopped
lemon juice to taste

Soak the oats in the orange juice overnight. Then add the rest of the prepared ingredients. Mix well and serve.

Handy hint: the fruit can be prepared overnight and mixed with the yoghourt in the morning if time is limited.

Fish Finger Wrap

Cooking time: 10 minutes
Dish: oval platter
Serves: 2

2 oz. cooking fat
2 slices bread, crusts removed
4 frozen fish fingers

4 rashers streaky bacon
2 tomatoes, halved

Fry the bread and keep warm on the dish. Fry the fish fingers for 2 minutes on each side. Wrap the bacon round the fish fingers, and fry for a further 2 minutes on each side. Fry the tomatoes at the same time. Put the fish fingers on the dish and then place the tomatoes at each end. Serve immediately.

Handy hint: stretch the rashers by scraping with the blade of a knife, before wrapping round each fish finger.

Sandwiched Grillburgers

Cooking time: 15 minutes
Dish: oval platter
Serves: 4

4 circles of bread, same size as grillburgers
1 egg, beaten

2 oz. margarine or butter
8 oz. frozen grillburgers
1 tomato, sliced

Soak the 4 circles of bread in the egg, then fry until crisp and golden each side. Place on serving dish and keep warm. Fry the grillburgers according to pack instructions. For the last 4 minutes, fry the tomato slices. Place the grillburgers on the bread, and then top each with a slice of tomato and serve.

Handy hint: be careful not to fry the grillburgers too quickly or they will lose their round shape.

Kipper Fluffs

Cooking time: 20–25 minutes
Oven: gas mark 7, 425°F
Dish: oval platter
Serves: 4
Colour picture page 17

12 oz. kipper fillets
4 slices of bread

2–3 oz. butter
4 eggs

Poach kipper fillets for 5–10 minutes. Trim off the crusts from bread, then butter on both sides. Place on a baking sheet. Mash fish until smooth adding a knob of butter. Separate eggs. Whisk the egg whites until stiff, then fold them into the fish. Divide equally and spread over the bread slices, leaving a deep 'well' in the centre. Drop one yolk into each 'well' and bake for 10 minutes. Garnish with parsley sprigs and serve immediately.

Handy hint: leave egg yolks in shells after separating: they then are easier to drop into each 'well'.

Sweet and Sour Gammon Rashers

Cooking time: 12–15 minutes
Dish: oval platter
Serves: 4

4 gammon rashers
juice 2 large oranges } mix
1 teaspoon clear honey } together

1 orange, skinned and sliced

Brush the gammon rashers liberally with the juice and grill each side for 4–5 minutes, under a pre-heated medium grill. Add the orange slices for the last 2–3 minutes of the cooking time. Serve the gammon rashers on the dish and place an orange slice on each rasher.

Handy hint: snip gammon fat with scissors, to prevent curling.

Farmhouse Eggs

Cooking time: 15 minutes
Dish: oval platter
Serves: 4

4 rashers streaky bacon, rind
  removed, chopped
1 onion, sliced into rings
1 oz. butter
4 pork sausages, skinned and
  halved

2 oz. mushrooms, sliced
2 tomatoes, chopped
4 eggs, beaten }
1 tablespoon 'top of milk' } mixed
seasoning

Fry the bacon until crisp and onion until it is soft. Add the butter and fry sausages for 5 minutes. Add mushrooms, tomatoes, then pour the egg mixture on top. Cook until it has set. Serve immediately.

Handy hint: fry all the ingredients carefully to prevent any tiny burnt pieces of food from colouring the beaten egg.

Smoked Haddock Omelette

Cooking time: 20 minutes
Dish: oval platter
Serves: 2

8 oz. smoked haddock fillet
2 eggs, separated
few drops of lemon juice
salt and pepper to taste

1 tablespoon parsley, chopped
½ oz. butter
lemon, parsley, *for garnish*

Poach the haddock for 8–10 minutes in milk and water. When cooked, skin and flake, adding a dab of butter. Add egg yolks, lemon juice, seasonings and parsley. Whisk the egg whites until stiff and fold into the fish mixture. Heat the butter in an omelette pan and pour in the fish mixture. Cook over a gentle heat until the underside is lightly browned, about 4 minutes, then brown the top under a hot grill. Serve at once garnished with lemon and parsley sprigs.

Handy hint: if using frozen fillets and cooking as pack instructions, add about 1 tablespoon lemon juice or vinegar to aluminium pans to prevent blackening.

Banana Brunch

Cooking time: 10 minutes
Dish: oval platter
Serves: 4

2 rashers bacon, halved
2 bananas, halved

11 oz. frozen steaklets
cooking oil

Wrap a piece of bacon around each half of banana. Brush with oil. Place the steaklets in the grill pan together with the bananas and grill under medium heat for 10 minutes, turning once.

Handy hint: streaky is better than back bacon, for rolling up.

Steaklet Scramble

Cooking time: 10 minutes
Dish: oval platter
Serves: 2

2 oz. cooking fat
5½ oz. frozen steaklets
2 small slices of bread

½ oz. butter
1 egg, beaten
1 tablespoon milk

Melt the fat, and fry the steaklets according to pack instructions, turning once. Remove the steaklets from fat and keep hot while frying the bread in the remaining fat. Meanwhile, melt the butter, add the egg and milk, then cook, stirring all the time. Serve steaklets on fried bread with scrambled egg on top. Garnish with a sprig of parsley, if liked.

Handy hint: be careful not to brown the butter before adding the egg, or it will not be a good yellow colour when scrambled.

Grapefruit Pancakes

Cooking time: 25–30 minutes
Dish: round platter
Serves: 4

pancakes
2 oz. batter mix
¼ pint milk
1 egg
1 dessertspoon cooking oil

1 grapefruit, segmented
½ pint frozen concentrated
    grapefruit juice, diluted
1 teaspoon arrowroot
sugar to taste

Make the pancakes. Place a few grapefruit segments on each pancake, and sprinkle with sugar to taste. Then fold the pancakes into quarters and arrange these attractively on the warmed dish. Blend the arrowroot with a little of the juice. Heat remaining juice, pour over arrowroot and return to saucepan, bring to the boil and allow sauce to thicken, then pour over pancakes and serve.

Handy hint: if making a number of pancakes pile them flat, one on top of the other, and cover. Keep warm. Fill and fold just before serving.

MID-WEEK MEALS AND SNACKS

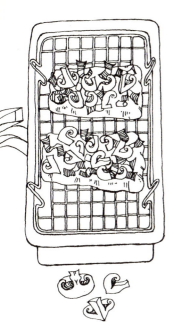

Mid-week meals are often more difficult to plan than those at the weekend because you may have to use food left over from the weekend. Also, our midday eating habits and types of work differ widely. School meals, office lunches or housework all affect our dietary requirements and our inclination to eat properly.

Daytime meals are often missed altogether or they may just be hurried snacks, deficient in some of the essential nutrients.

This section deals with meals suitable for working girls, below, busy mums on page 15, and family evening meals on page 11.

WORKING GIRLS

Whether you perch on a pivoting stool and swallow a ham roll in two mouthfuls, eat a piece of cheese and an apple at your desk, or savour the delights of canteen catering at lunchtime, you'll be tired when you eventually get home. So the evening meal must be quick, nourishing and sustaining.

Convenience foods can be invaluable to the working girl as they can solve so many of her problems. By always having a selection in store, shopping excursions can be reduced and quickly prepared meals will be no problem. Frozen fish, meat and vegetables, in particular, can all be used in portion quantities, leaving the remainder of the packets to be stored for future use. Reduced cooking time and fewer pots and pans to wash-up afterwards will enable you to make the most of your evening leisure time.

All the recipes in this section are simple to prepare and provide a balanced portion of the protein and vitamins we need for healthy eating.

Haddock Grill

Cooking time: 15 minutes
Dish: oval platter
Serves: 1—2

2 4-oz. pieces fresh or frozen
  haddock
1 rasher bacon, rind removed
  and chopped
1 oz. mushrooms, chopped
salt and pepper
watercress *for garnish*

Grill the haddock for about 12 minutes. Pile the bacon and mushrooms on top of the fish, season and grill for final 3 minutes.

Handy hint: serve garnished with watercress.

Fried Saucy Chicken

Cooking time: 30 minutes
Dish: oval or round platter
Serves: 1

1 chicken joint
butter for frying
sauce
a few onion rings
1 tomato, sliced
1 tablespoon tomato ketchup
1 teaspoon Worcestershire sauce
pinch mixed herbs
salt and pepper

Fry chicken joint gently in butter for 7 minutes on each side. Remove from the pan and keep warm. Fry the onion rings and tomato quickly, add the remaining sauce ingredients and heat through. Serve the chicken joint with the sauce poured over.

Handy hint: sliced green beans, sweet corn and potato crisps can be served to complete the meal.

Beefburger Nests

Cooking time: 20 minutes
Oven: gas mark 6, 400°F
Dish: oval ovenproof platter
Serves: 1–2

2 home-made hamburgers *or*
4 oz. frozen beefburgers

8 oz. potatoes, cooked and creamed
2 eggs

Place the beefburgers on an ovenproof platter. Pipe two layers of potato round the edge of each beefburger. Break the eggs individually into a cup, and tip one into each of the 'nests'. Bake until the potato is golden and the the egg is just set.

Handy hint: make sure that the two layers of potato are joined securely all round, to prevent egg white escaping.

Corned Beef Hash

Cooking time: 20 minutes
Oven: gas mark 6, 400°F
Dish: 1-pint flameproof casserole
Serves: 1–2

1 small onion, chopped finely
½ oz. butter
5 oz. can baked beans
7 oz. can corned beef, chopped

1 tomato, skinned
4 oz. frozen mixed vegetables
seasoning
1 potato, parboiled

Fry the onion in the butter, gently without browning, until soft. Add the beans, corned beef, tomato, mixed vegetables and seasoning. Mix thoroughly. Arrange slices of potato to cover the casserole and bake until crisp and golden.

Handy hint: if preferred, omit the potato and cook in a pan, as a stew.

Orange Snow

Cooking time: 5 minutes
Time to set
Dish: individual sundae glass
Serves: 1

½ oz. custard powder
2 teaspoons castor sugar
¼ pint milk

juice of 2 medium oranges
1 egg, separated

Blend the custard powder, sugar and milk together in a saucepan. Heat and stir until thick. Allow to cool slightly, then add the orange juice and egg yolk, stir well. Whisk the egg white until stiff and fold into the orange mixture. Pour into a glass dish and leave to set. Decorate with fresh cream if desired.

Handy hint: make sure that the egg white is very stiff before carefully folding into the mixture.

Mousse Parfait

Cooking time: nil
Dish: glass tumbler or tall sundae glass
Serves: 1

small frozen chocolate mousse
1 macaroon, crushed
2 pear halves, diced

3 tablespoons chocolate sauce
2 tablespoons chopped almonds,
   toasted

In a tall glass make alternate layers of spoonfuls of mousse and the remaining ingredients, ending with a sprinkling of nuts and a whirl of cream, if liked.

Handy hint: spoon the mousse into the glass while still hard.

FAMILY SUPPERS

You and your family need a well balanced diet to keep you lively and healthy. We tend to eat the foods we enjoy, so it's up to you as chief cook to make sure that any daytime deficiencies, when the family is left to its own devices, are put right by the evening meal.

The recipes which follow are simple to prepare and make excellent eating in the evening.

Cheesy Fish Fingers

Cooking time: 10 minutes
Dish: oval platter
Serves: 2–3

6 oz. frozen fish fingers
1 oz. cheese, grated
½ teaspoon dry mustard

parsley, chopped
½ oz. melted butter
seasoning

Grill the fish fingers on one side for 5 minutes. Meanwhile, mix remaining ingredients in a bowl. Turn fish fingers, spread some of mixture on each and grill for a further 5 minutes.

Handy hint: serve with grilled tomatoes and cooked frozen peas.

Savoury Haddock Pie

Cooking time: 45 minutes
Oven: gas mark 6, 400°F
Dish: 7-inch deep pie-plate
Serves: 4

8 oz. fillet smoked haddock
1 (2–3 serving) packet
  instant potato   potato
1 oz. butter   pastry
4 oz. plain flour
½ oz. butter
½ oz. flour

¼ pint milk
2 eggs, hard-boiled, shelled and
  chopped
1 tablespoon parsley, chopped
salt and pepper
beaten egg *to glaze*

Poach smoked haddock in milk and water for about 10–12 minutes; drain, reserving liquor. Prepare mashed potato, then stir in 1 oz. butter and gradually add the 4 oz. flour; allow the potato pastry to cool. Melt the ½ oz. butter in a pan and stir in the ½ oz. flour. Remove from heat, blend in the milk and return to the boil, stirring. Add the fish liquor, the skinned, flaked fish, chopped egg and parsley. Season well and pour into pie-plate. Roll out pastry on a floured surface and cover pie. Brush with egg glaze, then bake for 30 minutes. Serve hot.

Handy hint: pick up the delicate pastry by rolling it round the rolling pin. Unroll on to the top of the dish.

Fish Fingers with Jacket Potatoes

Cooking time: 1 hour
Oven: gas mark 6, 400°F
Dish: oval platter
Serves: 3

3 large potatoes
6 oz. frozen fish fingers

1 oz. butter
2 oz. cheese, grated

Scrub the potatoes, prick well and bake for 1 hour. Meanwhile, fry the fish fingers according to pack instructions. Split the potatoes in half, put a knob of butter on each, season, then place a fish finger on top of each half. Sprinkle with a little cheese and place under a hot grill to melt the cheese.

Handy hint: if you like to eat the potato skins, brush them with melted butter before baking.

Family Fish Supper Dish

Cooking time: 1 hour
Oven: gas mark 4, 350°F
Dish: greased, ovenproof dish
Serves: 4

1 lb. fresh or frozen cod fillet
milk, 1½ oz. butter
1 onion, peeled and chopped
1 small clove of garlic, crushed

1 oz. flour
1 tablespoon parsley, chopped
2—3 tomatoes, skinned, de-seeded
6 oz. packet instant potato

Poach the fish in a mixture of a little milk and water for 10–15 minutes, drain, reserving liquor. When cooked, flake the fish and place in the dish. Melt the butter and lightly fry the onion and crushed garlic until soft, without browning. Add the flour, off the heat. Make the fish liquor up to ½ pint with milk and stir into pan. Return to the heat and bring to the boil, stirring. Season, pour over the fish and arrange the tomatoes on top. Cover with the mashed potato and bake for 35 minutes.

Handy hint: to crush garlic, use a garlic press or flat blade of a knife.

Beefburger Bean Bake

Cooking time: 30 minutes
Oven: gas mark 5, 375°F
Dish: shallow ovenproof casserole
Serves: 4

16 oz. can baked beans
1 oz. margarine
4 home-made hamburgers or 8 oz.
   frozen beefburgers with onion

1 large onion, sliced
4 oz. button mushrooms, peeled

Place the beans in the dish. Melt margarine in a pan, add beefburgers with the onion and mushrooms; fry gently for 5 minutes turning once. Remove beefburgers and place on the beans. Cook vegetables for a further 3 minutes, drain; place mushrooms on beefburgers and onion rings on top. Bake for 15–20 minutes. Serve at once.

Handy hint: when fried, drain beefburgers, etc., on kitchen paper.

Savoury Rice Steaklets

Cooking time: 20 minutes
Dish: round or oval platter
Serves: 4

1 oz. butter
1 onion, chopped
2 rashers bacon, chopped
6 oz. long grain rice
¾ pint water

2 tablespoons tomato ketchup
½ level teaspoon mixed herbs
salt and pepper
11 oz. frozen steaklets

Melt the butter in a saucepan, fry onion, bacon and rice gently for 3 minutes. Add water, ketchup, herbs and seasoning. Bring to the boil, stirring constantly, then cover and simmer for 15 minutes until the rice is cooked and water absorbed. Place in a serving dish and keep hot. Meanwhile, cook the steaklets; serve on the savoury rice.

Handy hint: the steaklets could be grilled or fried for this recipe.

Sweet Corn Supper Savoury

Cooking time: 20 minutes
Dish: oval platter
Serves: 4

6 oz. sweet corn, canned or frozen
1–2 oz. cooking fat
4 large slices bread
1 oz. butter
1 small onion, chopped
2 oz. button mushrooms, sliced
7 oz. can pork luncheon meat,
    cut into ¼-inch cubes
2 teaspoons Worcestershire sauce
salt and pepper

Cook the sweet corn for 5–10 minutes. Meanwhile, melt the fat and fry the bread on both sides. Remove bread slices and place on a serving dish. Add butter, onion, mushrooms and luncheon meat to the pan. Fry gently for 5 minutes, add sweet corn and stir in Worcestershire sauce and seasoning. Divide equally between the four slices of bread; serve garnished with tomato and watercress.

Handy hint: over-cooked sweet corn toughens.

Farmhouse Pie

Cooking time: 35 minutes
Oven: gas mark 7, 425°F
Dish: 2-pint pie dish
Serves: 4–5
Colour picture, page 20

1 oz. butter
4 rashers steaky bacon, rind
    removed, chopped
1 onion, chopped finely
6 oz. can condensed cream of
    mushroom soup
¼ pint stock
6 oz. sweet corn, canned or frozen
12 oz. cooked chicken meat
½ tablespoon parsley, chopped
7½ oz. frozen puff pastry, thawed
beaten egg *to glaze*

Melt butter in a pan and fry the bacon and onion gently for 5 minutes. Stir in the condensed soup and stock and bring to the boil. Add corn and cubed chicken meat, season well and add the parsley. Pour into pie dish and allow to cool. Roll out the pastry on a floured surface and cover the pie. Flute edges of the pastry, and roll out trimmings to make 'leaves' for decoration. Glaze well and make a hole in centre to allow steam to escape. Bake until golden brown.

Handy hint: try to use a 2-pint pie dish so that the pastry is supported by the filling. Otherwise use a pie-raiser.

Fluffy Cheese and Onion Flan

Cooking time: 40 minutes
Oven: gas mark 6, 400°F
Tin: 8-inch flan ring
Serves: 4–5

4 oz. short crust pastry (or
    7½ oz. frozen, thawed)
5 oz. frozen small onions and
    white sauce
4 oz. cheese, grated
2 eggs, separated
salt and pepper

Roll out the pastry and line the flan ring. Cover the base of the flan with greaseproof paper and bake 'blind'. Bake for 15 minutes. Remove the greaseproof paper. Meanwhile, cook the onions and white sauce as pack instructions. Add 3 oz. of the cheese and the egg yolks. Whisk the egg whites and fold into the mixture. Pour into the flan case and sprinkle top with the remaining cheese. Bake for 25 minutes.

Handy hint: to bake 'blind', line the pastry case with greaseproof paper and cover with a layer of dried beans, rice or macaroni.

Banana and Nut Gâteau

Cooking time: nil
Time to thaw
Dish: round platter
Serves: 6

1 frozen dairy cream sponge
2 bananas
juice of half lemon

1 teaspoon castor sugar
3 tablespoons walnuts, chopped

While the sponge is still frozen, slice horizontally through the cream. Leave the two halves to partially thaw at room temperature (approximately 1 hour). Slice three-quarters of 1 banana into rings and toss in a little lemon juice. Mash the remaining banana with sugar and the rest of the lemon juice, stir in about half the nuts and spread this mixture over one half of the sponge. Put remaining half of the sponge, cream-side uppermost, on top and sprinkle centre with remainder of nuts. Arrange overlapping rings of banana round the edge, place half a walnut in centre and serve.

Handy hint: toss banana in lemon juice immediately to keep white.

Orange Rice Meringue

Cooking time:
base: 25 minutes
meringue: 5 minutes
Oven: gas mark 5, 375°F
Dish: 2-pint oval pie dish
Serves: 6

11 oz. can mandarin oranges, drained
juice from mandarin oranges and water to make 1 pint
2 oz. long grain rice

2 egg yolks
juice of 2 medium oranges
2 egg whites
2 oz. castor sugar } meringue
6 orange segments

Arrange oranges in base of dish. Pour liquid into pan, and bring to boil. Add rice and cook for 17 minutes. Add eggs and orange juice and stir over gentle heat for 3 minutes. Pour over fruit. Whisk egg whites stiffly and fold in sugar. Pile on top of rice and place in oven. Serve hot, decorated with orange segments.

Handy hint: meringue will be browned after 5 minutes; it should be soft inside.

Pear and Ginger Flan

Cooking time: 40 minutes
Oven: gas mark 5, 375°F
Tin: 7-inch flan ring
Serves: 5–6

4 oz. short crust pastry (or 7½ oz. frozen, thawed)
15 oz. can pear halves
3 oz. plain flour
1½ oz. margarine

2 oz. demerara sugar
1 oz. walnuts, chopped
1 oz. porridge oats
1½ oz. preserved ginger, chopped finely

Line the flan ring with the pastry. Strain the syrup from the pears and arrange the fruit over the bottom of the flan. Rub the margarine into the flour then add the remaining dry ingredients and the ginger. Sprinkle over the pears. Bake.

Handy hint: press pastry firmly into bottom of flan ring. Any air trapped will expand during baking and push out the pastry, etc.

LUNCH FOR BUSY MUMS

All on your own at midday? How tempting it is to 'make do' with a cup of tea and a few biscuits, a can of soup or a sticky bun!

Why not give yourself a treat, every day, with only a *little* extra effort? These tasty, nourishing snacks will relieve the pangs of hunger, sustain you for the day's tasks, and supply a good proportion of the proteins and vitamins you need as much as everyone else.

Kipper Rarebit

Cooking time: 20 minutes
Dish: warmed plates
Serves: 2

6 oz. kipper fillets
butter
2 large slices of bread

3 tomatoes, sliced
3 oz. cheese, grated

Poach the kippers for 5 minutes, drain and add a knob of butter. Toast the bread and arrange tomato on each slice. Cover with half the cheese and grill until it begins to melt. Arrange the kipper fillets on top and cover with the remaining cheese. Grill for a further 4–5 minutes before serving.

Handy hint: make sure the grill is really hot to melt the cheese.

Cod Steaks in Yoghourt Sauce

Cooking time: 15 minutes
Dish: oval platter
Serves: 1

1 cod steak (or $3\frac{1}{2}$ oz. frozen)
2 tablespoons natural yoghourt
1 egg yolk

pinch of dry mustard
little parsley, chopped *for garnish*

Poach the cod steak in a little milk and water for 5–7 minutes. Drain and place in a warmed serving dish. Heat yoghourt very slowly in a saucepan. Mix the egg yolk with the mustard, and add to the yoghourt in the pan. Stir over low heat until the sauce thickens. Season to taste. Pour sauce over steak, garnish with parsley.

Handy hint: drain the cod steak on crumpled kitchen paper.

Brunchburgers

Cooking time: 20 minutes
Dish: oval platter
Serves: 1–2

2 oz. cooking fat
2 small slices bread, crusts removed
4 oz. frozen beefburgers with onion

1 tomato, cut in half
2 4-inch strips of bacon
1 oz. cheese, grated

Melt the fat in a frying pan and fry the bread on both sides until golden brown; place bread in grill pan. Fry the beefburgers in the pan. When cooked, place each on a slice of bread, and top with a tomato half and bacon strip. Grill for 2 minutes. Sprinkle with grated cheese and continue grilling until the cheese is golden.

Handy hint: fry beefburgers gently to retain their round shape.

Beefburger Curry

Cooking time: 30 minutes
Dish: round plate
Serves: 1

1 oz. margarine
½ small onion, chopped finely
1 small apple, peeled, cored and
    chopped finely
2 teaspoons curry powder
1 level tablespoon flour
¼ pint stock

salt and pepper
1 teaspoon lemon juice
1 tablespoon chutney
1½ oz. long grain rice
4 oz. frozen beefburgers with
    onion *or* 2 home-made
    hamburgers, well seasoned

Melt the margarine in a saucepan, fry the onion and apple gently until lightly browned. Stir in the curry powder and flour, and cook for 2 minutes. Add the stock, tomato, seasoning, lemon juice and chutney. Bring to the boil, cover and simmer for 20 minutes. Meanwhile, boil the rice in salted water for about 15 minutes and drain. Fry the beefburgers for 5 minutes each side. Arrange rice round edge of serving plate, place the beefburgers in centre, pour the sauce over.

Handy hint: cook rice without a lid on pan to prevent boiling over.

Hawaiian Steaklets

Cooking time: 10 minutes
Dish: individual ovenproof dish
Serves: 1
Colour picture, page 28

5½ oz. frozen steaklets
half 8½ oz. can pineapple rings

4 oz. frozen sliced green beans
tomato slices *for garnish*

Grill steaklets according to pack instructions and place on warmed serving dish. Grill the pineapple rings and tomato until heated through. Cook the beans; drain and place around the edges of the steaklets. Garnish with pineapple rings and tomato wedges.

Handy hint: grill steaklets under medium heat to prevent curling.

Spanish Omelette

Cooking time: 15 minutes
Dish: oval plate
Serves: 1

½ oz. butter
½ small onion, sliced
1 tomato, sliced
2 oz. frozen peas

salt and pepper
pinch mixed herbs
2 eggs, beaten

Melt the butter in a frying pan. Add the onion, tomato, peas and seasoning and fry gently for 2–3 minutes. Add the eggs to the pan and stir over gentle heat until the egg is firm. Fold over and serve on a hot plate.

Handy hint: to make this omelette more substantial, some leftover potato can be added with the other vegetables.

Chocolate Mousse with Ginger and Nut Sauce

Cooking time: nil
Dish: small round glass dish or
saucer
Serves: 1

frozen chocolate tub mousse
1 piece stem ginger, chopped
½ oz. walnuts, chopped

1 tablespoon ginger syrup
1 teaspoon water

Turn out the mousse on to an individual serving dish. Mix the sauce ingredients together and pour over.

Handy hint: turn out the mousse while frozen. If necessary, dip into hot water to loosen from the mould.

Kipper Fluffs, for recipe see page 7

STOP-THE-CLOCK COOKERY

for the days when you don't know what time they're arriving

Like people, some dishes demand punctuality. Others are more easy going. Rather than have your creative efforts spoiled by a 'phone call announcing a late arrival, take advantage of some of the recipes in this section.

When your husband is kept at the office, your family are uncertain what time they'll be in, or your visitors are the sort that always turn up late, these recipes can do wonders for any hostess or busy mum.

All the recipes can be partially cooked or prepared, and either reheated or finished in a short time. Some are cold, substantial dishes which can be kept waiting for some time.

Each recipe is marked with a stopwatch symbol like this Ö to indicate the best place at which to stop the clock.

STOPWATCH FAMILY DISHES

Haddock Chowder

Cooking time: 20 minutes
Dish: individual soup bowls
Serves: 6

1 lb. fresh or frozen fillet haddock
1 pint stock
1 teaspoon salt
1 lb. 3 oz. can potatoes, drained and diced
½ oz. butter
3 rashers streaky bacon, rind removed, chopped
1 large onion, chopped
½ pint milk
black pepper
parsley *for garnish*

Cook the fish in the simmering stock for 10 minutes. Remove the fish, skin and flake then return to the fish liquor. Add the drained, diced potato. Meanwhile, melt the butter and sauté the bacon and onion until the onion is transparent. Add to the fish broth, together with the milk and seasoning. Ö Heat slowly to simmering point, but do not boil. Serve garnished with a little chopped parsley.

Handy hint: serve croûtes of toast as an accompaniment. Alternatively, fry bacon rinds until very crisp, drain and crush for a garnish.

Green Pea Soup

Cooking time: 15 minutes
Dish: casserole or soup tureen
Serves: 4

8 oz. shelled peas (or frozen)
¾ oz. margarine
¾ oz. flour
1 pint milk
salt and pepper
2 teaspoons lemon juice
little single cream
nutmeg, if liked
} *for garnish*

Cook the peas in ½ pint boiling salted water for 5 minutes. Rub the peas and water through a fine sieve. Meanwhile, melt the margarine in a saucepan, add the flour to make a roux, remove from the heat and gradually add the milk, stirring. Bring to the boil, continue stirring, and cook for 2 minutes. Season the sauce, then add the pea purée and mix well. Ö Reheat, when required. Just before serving, mix in the lemon juice. Serve garnished with a swirl of cream and a sprinkling of nutmeg.

Handy hint: the peas and cooking water can be puréed in a liquidiser if preferred.

Fish Puffs

Cooking time: 40 minutes
Time to chill
Oven: gas mark 7, 425°F
Dish: oval platter
Serves: 4

1 oz. butter
1 small onion, chopped finely
4 oz. mushrooms, chopped
½ tablespoon parsley, chopped

salt and pepper
13 oz. frozen puff pastry, thawed
4 frozen cod steaks
beaten egg *to glaze*

Melt the butter, add onion and fry gently for 3 minutes, add mushrooms and cook for a further 3 minutes. Add parsley, season well, then allow to cool. Roll out the pastry to measure 14 × 12 inches, and cut into four 7 × 6-inch pieces. Place a cod steak in centre of each piece and divide the mushroom mixture between them. Damp edges of the pastry, fold over to enclose fish and seal ends and edges. Place puffs on a baking sheet, sealed edges downwards, then brush with egg and make two slits on the top. Chill. ⏲ Bake for about 30 minutes until pastry is risen and well browned.

Handy hint: make sure vegetable mixture is cold before making puffs, or you will melt the pastry fat and prevent it rising properly.

Beefburger and Noodle Stroganoff

Cooking time: 10 minutes
Dish: large rectangular casserole
Serves: 4

2 oz. butter
1 onion, chopped
1 clove of garlic, chopped
4 oz. mushrooms, sliced
4 home-made hamburgers *or* 8 oz. frozen beefburgers

2 tablespoons tomato purée
⅛ pint beef stock
seasoning
⅛ pint sour cream
4 oz. noodles
2 oz. cheese, grated

Melt butter and fry onion and garlic (2 minutes). Add mushrooms and beefburgers and fry gently. ⏲ Later, blend tomato purée with stock, seasoning and cream; add to pan and reheat. Cook noodles in boiling salted water. Drain and place in dish. Arrange beefburgers on noodles and pour over sauce. Sprinkle with grated cheese and grill until golden brown. Serve garnished with parsley.

Handy hint: cook noodles in a pan without lid to prevent boiling over. Drain in nylon sieve.

Steaklets Italienne

Cooking time: 20 minutes
Dish: shallow casserole
Serves: 4

sauce
1 oz. butter
1 small onion, chopped finely
¼ teaspoon garlic, minced
1 level tablespoon flour
8 oz. can tomatoes
1 beef stock cube, dissolved in
    ¼ pint boiling water
1 teaspoon tomato purée
pinch of sugar, seasoning

11 oz. frozen steaklets
4 oz. spaghetti

Melt the butter in a pan, add onion and garlic and soften gently. Stir in the flour until smooth. Add tomatoes, stock, purée and sugar; bring to the boil and simmer for 5 minutes. Season. ⏲ Later, grill the steaklets as pack instructions. Cook the spaghetti in boiling salted water until soft; drain, then put in the casserole, pour sauce down the centre and arrange steaklets on top.

Handy hint: cook spaghetti in a pan without lid to prevent boiling over. To give shine, add a knob of butter and toss before serving.

Farmhouse Pie, for recipe see page 13

Chicken Napoli, for recipe see page 34

Titania Chicken Salad

Cooking time: 30 minutes
Dish: round platter or salad bowl
Serves: 4

1 large or 2 small spring
    chicken cut into 4 joints
butter for frying
2 oz. long grain rice
8 oz. black grapes, halved and
    pips removed

3 oz. salted almonds, chopped
    coarsely
2 eggs, hard-boiled and chopped
pinch of salt, pepper, sugar and
    dry mustard
2 tablespoons olive oil
1 tablespoon wine vinegar

Fry chicken joints gently until tender, in a little butter; about 10–15 minutes each side. Boil the rice, Cool both. Mix the grapes, almonds, rice and eggs together. Place the seasonings in a bowl, add the oil, then stir in the vinegar, gradually. Add to rice mixture. 🕑 Pile on a dish and arrange chicken joints on top.

Handy hint: serve with lettuce and tomato.

Grapefruit Crumb Pie

Cooking time: 25 minutes
Oven: gas mark 6, 400°F
Dish: 8-inch flan ring, fluted
Serves: 4–6

4 oz. short crust pastry (or
    7½ oz. frozen, thawed)
2 oz. ground almonds
2 oz. wholemeal biscuits, crushed
2 oz. castor sugar

½ 6¼ fl. oz. can frozen
    concentrated grapefruit
    juice, thawed
1 tablespoon milk
2 eggs, separated

Roll out pastry and line flan ring. Mix together remaining ingredients, except egg white. 🕑 Fold the stiffly whisked egg white into mixture carefully. Pile into flan case and bake.

Handy hint: be careful not to stretch the pastry while lining the flan ring, or it will shrink during cooking.

Mousse Delight

Cooking time: 5 minutes
Dish: individual sundae glasses
Serves: 3

1 oz. sugar
¼ pint water
2 oz. plain chocolate
1 level teaspoon cornflour, blended
    with a little of the water
juice of 1 orange

1 orange, peeled and segmented
    with all the pith removed
9 oz. frozen chocolate mousse,
    partially thawed
¼ oz. flaked almonds

In a small pan, dissolve the sugar in the water, then add the chocolate and simmer for 3 minutes until it is dissolved. Stir in the blended cornflour, bring to the boil and cook for 2 minutes. 🕑 Leave the sauce to cool, then add the juice from the orange. Spoon the mousse into 3 individual sundae glasses, with the orange segments, and pour over the cooled sauce. Decorate with a few flaked almonds.

Handy hint: avoid boiling the chocolate mixture; this sometimes produces lumps.

Pescadao en Avellana

Cooking time: 40 minutes
Time to stand: 30 minutes
Oven: gas mark 6, 400°F
Dish: shallow ovenproof dish
Serves: 4

4 fresh or frozen cod steaks
1 tablespoon lemon juice
salt and pepper
1½ oz. butter, melted
3 oz. hazelnuts, chopped finely
   or ground

1½ oz. cheese, grated
1 tablespoon sherry
3 tablespoons milk
3 tablespoons fresh white
   breadcrumbs
pinch of nutmeg

Place cod steaks in the well greased dish. Sprinkle the fish with the lemon juice, season with salt and pepper, and allow to stand for ½ hour. 🕛 Later, brush with half of the melted butter. Mix the nuts and cheese with the sherry and milk and spread a portion of the mixture on each steak, covering the top completely. Sprinkle with the breadcrumbs, seasoned with salt and pepper and a pinch of nutmeg. Pour over the remaining butter, then bake.

Handy hint: after sprinkling the fish with lemon juice and seasoning, cover dish with foil and chill. Prepare the rest of the ingredients for swift action later.

Cod Steaks Provençale

Cooking time: 30 minutes
Oven: gas mark 5, 375°F
Dish: ovenproof dish
Serves: 4

4 fresh or frozen cod steaks
¼ bottle dry white wine
1 medium onion, chopped
8 oz. can tomatoes

pinch minced garlic
freshly ground pepper
salt

Marinate the cod steaks in the wine for a couple of hours. For the sauce, lightly fry the onion, add the tomatoes, garlic and seasoning. 🕛 Later, strain the liquor from the fish and add to the sauce. Place cod steaks in the dish, pour the sauce over. Bake for 20—25 minutes.

Handy hint: to prevent the wine evaporating cover closely with foil.

Cabillaud en Papillote

Cooking time: 30 minutes
Oven: gas mark 5, 375°F
Tin: baking sheet
Serves: 4

1 oz. butter
2 medium sized leeks (white part
   only) *or* onions, sliced finely
8 oz. tomatoes, skinned and de-
   seeded
4 oz. mushrooms, sliced
4 cod steaks

salt and pepper
2 tablespoons dry white wine *or*
   cider
6 oz. long grain rice
3 gherkins, sliced
1 tablespoon parsley, chopped

Melt the butter, add the leeks and cook gently, without browning, until tender. Add the tomatoes and mushrooms and cook gently for 2—3 minutes. Season well. Place each cod steak on a square of foil, large enough to fold over the fish. Season. Place a quarter of the vegetable mixture on each cod steak. Baste with the wine or cider. Fold over the foil to make a 'parcel'. Place on a baking sheet. 🕛 Later, bake for 20—25 minutes. Meanwhile, cook the rice in boiling salted water for 10 minutes. Drain, add gherkins and parsley, then pile on to serving dish. Remove foil and arrange fish on the rice.

Handy hint: to clean leeks, slit open to within 2 inches of the root. Open out and wash thoroughly under a cold tap.

Gâteau Moya, for recipe see page 54

Orange and Chocolate Soufflés, for recipe see page 27

Chicken and Asparagus Salad

Cooking time: nil
Dish: oval or round platter
Serves: 3–4

7 oz. can asparagus tips
3 cooked chicken joints
1 eating apple, peeled and cored

$\frac{1}{4}$ pint mayonnaise
lettuce

Strain the asparagus and put a few tips to one side for garnish. Strip the chicken from the bone, then dice. Mix the chicken, diced apple, asparagus and mayonnaise. Serve on a bed of lettuce and garnish with a few asparagus tips.

Handy hint: a quick mayonnaise; put a whole egg, seasoning and 1 tablespoon vinegar in liquidiser, switch on, gradually pour in up to $\frac{1}{4}$ pint oil, until mixture thickens.

Paella

Cooking time: 35 minutes
Dish: paella dish or round
entrée dish
Serves: 4
Colour picture, page 29

2 oz. butter
1 tablespoon oil
1 large onion, chopped finely
2 cloves of garlic, crushed
2 sticks celery
8 oz. long grain rice
1 pint chicken stock (made with
    a stock cube)

1 packet saffron powder
small can red peppers (pimientos),
    cut into strips
5 oz. shelled peas (or frozen)
12 oz. cooked chicken meat
4 oz. peeled prawns
salt, pepper, oregano (optional)

Melt the butter, add the oil, then fry the onion, garlic and celery. Cook until soft, without browning. Add the rice and cook for a minute, then add the chicken stock and saffron powder. Simmer *very* gently for about 15 minutes or until rice has absorbed the stock, then add remaining ingredients and heat for about 5 minutes.

Handy hint: if saffron is not available, use a pinch of turmeric powder to colour the rice.

Bacon and Onion Flan

Cooking time: 40 minutes
Oven: gas mark 6, 400°F
Tin: 7–8-inch flan ring
Serves: 4–6

4 rashers steaky bacon, rind
    removed and chopped
5 oz. frozen small onions and
    white sauce

salt and pepper
2 eggs, separated
4 oz. short crust pastry (or
    $7\frac{1}{2}$ oz. frozen, thawed)

Fry the bacon gently in a pan for 2–3 minutes. Add the onions and the given amount of water. Stir together until boiling, simmer gently for 5 minutes. Remove from the heat and stir in the seasoning and egg yolks. Meanwhile, roll out the pastry and line the flan ring. Later, reheat the onion mixture, whisk the egg whites and fold into onion mixture; pour into the flan case. Bake until set; the top will be well browned.

Handy hint: make sure that the egg whites are whisked very stiffly before folding into the rather heavy mixture.

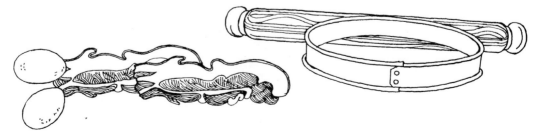

Festive Mould

Cooking time: nil
Mould: 1½-pint
Serves: 4

8 oz. fresh raspberries, or
    frozen, just thawed
1 packet lemon jelly

1 teaspoon lemon rind, grated
2 tablespoons lemon juice
½ pint double cream

Sprinkle fresh fruit with a little sugar, drain juice and heat; dissolve the jelly in this and then make up to ¾ pint with cold water. Add the lemon rind and juice and leave to cool. When nearly on the point of setting, whisk until light and fluffy. Whip three-quarters of the cream lightly and fold into the whisked jelly, with the raspberries. Turn into a mould and allow to set. ⓧ To serve, turn out, whip remaining cream and decorate with this.

Handy hint: turn out the jelly by dipping the mould into *hot* water for a few seconds. Place a plate upside down over the mould and invert.

Banana Rhumba

Cooking time: 10 minutes
Dish: round earthenware dish
Serves: 6

2 tablespoons undiluted frozen
    orange juice
½ pint water
1 oz. sugar
1 tablespoon golden syrup
1 oz. butter

6 medium bananas
1 tablespoon plain flour
1 tablespoon rum *or* cointreau
1 oz. almonds, blanched, cut into
    slivers and toasted

Place the orange juice, water, sugar, syrup and butter in a small frying pan. ⓧ Bring to the boil. Peel the bananas and cut in half, coat with flour and place in the boiling syrup. Reduce the heat and cook for a few minutes until tender. Lift bananas from the syrup and place on a serving dish. Add the rum or cointreau to the syrup. Bring back to the boil and pour over the bananas. Sprinkle with almonds and serve with cream or ice cream.

Handy hint: peel the bananas immediately before cooking so that they remain white.

Orange and Chocolate Soufflé

Cooking time: 5 minutes
Dish: 5-inch soufflé dish
or individual dishes
Serves: 4
Colour picture, page 25

4 oz. plain chocolate
3 oz. castor sugar
3 eggs, separated
¼–½ oz. gelatine

¼ pint water
3 tablespoons undiluted frozen
    orange juice
¼ pint double cream

Melt chocolate in a basin over a pan of hot water. Whisk egg yolks and sugar in a large basin over hot water until thick, fold in the melted chocolate. Dissolve the gelatine in the water over heat, then add with the orange juice to the chocolate mixture. Lightly whip the cream and fold in. Whisk egg whites until stiff and fold into mixture. Pour into the soufflé dish, prepared with a foil collar, or into individual glass dishes, and leave to set. ⓧ Remove collar and decorate with extra whipped cream before serving.

Handy hint: make collar for the soufflé dish by cutting a piece of foil 3 inches taller than soufflé dish and pressing it round side. Smooth top into a perfect circle before filling the dish.

Hawaiian Steaklets, for recipe see page 16

Paella, for recipe see page 26

I HATE WASHING UP

Whether you hate washing-up or just like one-pot cookery, there are many occasions when it is very convenient to have a tasty meal which requires little or no attention and few utensils.

Usually, recipes for one-pot cookery take a little longer to cook but this is offset by the short preparation and washing-up time.

Ovenproof casseroles with well fitting lids are essential for this type of cooking. If they can be used on top of the cooker, they can serve as a sauté dish as well. Meat or chicken joints which require browning can be fried in the same dish, and the tasty juices and browned vegetables all conserved to add flavour and colour. Remember too, a shallow casserole with a large area for frying is usually more useful than a deep pot.

In this section, you will also find recipes which require no cooking and some which are cooked in the oven in a pie dish or baking tin. A pressure cooker can be used for the casserole recipes, allowing one-third the suggested cooking time.

Kipper Quiche

Cooking time:
pastry: 15 minutes
filling: 20 minutes
Oven:
pastry: gas mark 6, 400°F
filling: gas mark 5, 375°F
Dish: large round platter
Serves: 4—5

12 oz. kipper fillets	2 eggs
4 oz. short crust pastry (or	$\frac{1}{4}$ pint milk
7$\frac{1}{2}$ oz. frozen, thawed)	pepper to taste

Poach kippers for 10 minutes. Drain, reserve liquor; skin and flake kippers finely adding a pat of butter. Roll out pastry to fit a 7-inch square or 8-inch round shallow tin. Line pastry with greaseproof paper and cover base with uncooked rice or dried beans. Bake for 10 minutes. Remove paper and beans, return to oven and bake case for a further 5 minutes. Beat eggs lightly in a basin, add milk, fish, and seasonings. Spoon filling into pastry case. Reduce oven temperature and bake until filling is set.

Handy hint: serve hot or cold with a tossed green salad.

Cod Cobbler

Cooking time: 30—35 minutes
Oven: gas mark 6, 400°F
Dish: shallow greased ovenproof dish
Serves: 4

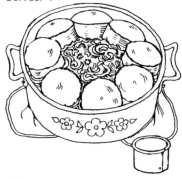

1 oz. margarine *or* butter	salt and pepper
1 onion, chopped	4 frozen cod steaks
6 oz. can condensed tomato soup	8 oz. self-raising flour
8 oz. can baked beans in tomato	pinch of salt
sauce	1$\frac{1}{2}$ oz. margarine
$\frac{1}{4}$ pint water	$\frac{1}{4}$ pint milk
1 tablespoon Worcestershire sauce	beaten egg *or* milk *to glaze scones*

Melt the margarine or butter in a pan and fry the onion gently for 5 minutes. Add the soup, baked beans, water and Worcestershire sauce and bring to the boil, stirring. Season well. Place cod steaks in the dish and pour the tomato mixture over. Mix the flour and salt together in a basin and rub in the margarine. Add the milk and knead the dough lightly before turning out on to a floured surface. Roll out until $\frac{1}{2}$-inch thick; cut out eight circles with a 2$\frac{1}{2}$—3-inch cutter, or cut into eight sections. Arrange these around outside of the dish, glaze with beaten egg or milk and bake until fish is cooked and the scones are risen.

Handy hint: serve with peas, sweet corn: cook, wrapped in foil, for 15—20 minutes. Season well; add knob of butter to each parcel.

Sunshine Cod

Cooking time: 30 minutes
Oven: gas mark 6, 400°F
Dish: ovenproof casserole
Serves: 4

13 oz. frozen cod fillet
1 teaspoon dry mustard
3 tablespoons mayonnaise
1 small onion, chopped finely
1 teaspoon lemon juice
½ teaspoon thyme
1 medium cooking apple, peeled, cored and chopped finely
seasoning
parsley *for garnish*

Skin fillets and cover base of casserole with fish. Mix other ingredients, then spread over fish. Cover with foil and bake. Garnish with parsley.

Handy hint: this is delicious served with a tossed green salad.

Haddock Soufflé

Cooking time: 30–35 minutes
Oven: gas mark 6, 400°F
Dish: 5–6-inch soufflé dish, greased
Serves: 2

8 oz. fresh or frozen fillet haddock
1 oz. margarine ⎫
1 oz. flour ⎬ sauce
¼ pint milk ⎭
1 tablespoon parsley, chopped
salt and pepper
3 eggs, separated

Poach the haddock steaks for about 12–15 minutes. Make a thick white sauce with the margarine, flour and milk and cook for 2 minutes. Add the flaked fish and parsley to the sauce then beat in the egg yolks and season well. Whisk the egg whites until they are stiff and gently fold into the fish mixture. Pour into the prepared soufflé dish and bake until risen and set.

Handy hint: make the egg whites *very* stiff before folding in.

Crispy Fish Pie

Cooking time: 45 minutes
Oven: gas mark 3, 325°F
Dish: greased 2-pint ovenproof dish
Serves: 4

4 fresh or frozen fillets plaice
1 oz. butter *or* margarine
1 onion, sliced into rings
8 oz. tomatoes, skinned and chopped
3 oz. mushrooms, sliced
½ oz. cheese, grated
½ oz. fresh white breadcrumbs
2 eggs
½ pint milk
pinch of herbs
1½ oz. fresh breadcrumbs ⎫
1½ oz. cheese, grated ⎬ topping
pinch of herbs ⎭

Remove the dark skin from fillets, fold them in half and place in the dish. Fry the onion in butter until translucent, add the tomatoes and mushrooms and fry for a further 3–4 minutes. Remove pan from heat and stir in the cheese and breadcrumbs. Pour mixture on to fish. Beat the eggs and milk, add the herbs and pour into the dish. To make topping, mix cheese, breadcrumbs and herbs and sprinkle over. Bake for 40 minutes. Before serving, grill to brown the topping.

Handy hint: to remove skin from fillets, place skin-side down and, starting from the tail end, gently lift the flesh from the skin, using the back of a knife.

31

Tuna and Cheese Pasties

Cooking time: 20 minutes
Oven: gas mark 7, 425°F
Tin: baking sheet
Serves: 5

3½ oz. can tuna fish
1 tablespoon vinegar
1 oz. cheese, grated
2 oz. shelled peas (or frozen)

1 small egg
salt and pepper
7½ oz. frozen puff pastry, thawed
milk *to glaze*

Place the tuna fish in a bowl, flake, add the vinegar, cheese, peas and egg; mix well together, season. Roll out the pastry thinly and using a 4-inch plain cutter, cut out five circles. Use a slightly larger cutter to cut five more circles for the top of the pasties. Place the 4-inch circles on a baking sheet and divide the mixture among them. Damp all around the edges and cover with the larger circles of pastry. Seal, and flake the edges with the back of a knife; flute, then glaze the pasties with milk. Make a slit in the top, and using the pastry trimmings, make pastry leaves to decorate. Bake. Serve hot or cold.

Handy hint: to re-roll scraps of pastry, place them evenly on top of each other. This will retain the air layers in the pastry and ensure even-rising during baking.

Devonshire Plait

Cooking time: 30 minutes
Oven: gas mark 6, 400°F
Tin: baking sheet
Serves: 6—8

4 oz. short crust pastry (or
  7½ oz. frozen, thawed)
6 oz. sweet corn, canned or frozen
4 oz. cooked minced beef *or*
  2 frozen beefburgers, chopped

2 oz. mushrooms, chopped
2 tablespoons tomato chutney
seasoning
1 egg, beaten

Roll out pastry to rectangle 12 × 9 inches, place on greased baking sheet. Down the long sides cut 1-inch wide strips, 2 inches in from edge. Mix together sweet corn, meat, mushrooms and chutney; season and add half the beaten egg. Pile mixture down centre of pastry, fold strips over this, alternately, crossing in centre to form plait. Brush over with remaining beaten egg and bake.

Handy hint: try not to stretch the pastry strips while making the plait. Stretched pastry shrinks back during baking.

Orange Pork Chops

Cooking time 1 hour 20 minutes
Dish: casserole
Serves: 4

2 tablespoons oil *or* fat
4 loin pork chops
1 onion, chopped
1 small apple, peeled, cored and
  chopped
1 tablespoon flour

1 chicken stock cube dissolved in
  ½ pint hot water
½ can undiluted frozen concentrated
  orange juice, thawed
salt and pepper

Heat oil or fat in a large saucepan and fry chops on both sides until brown, remove from pan. Add chopped onion and apple to pan and fry gently for 3 minutes. Remove pan from heat and stir in flour. Blend in remaining ingredients, return to heat and stir until sauce thickens and boils. Add chops to sauce, cover and simmer for 1 hour or until meat is tender. Adjust seasoning before serving.

Handy hint: this is easier to eat if the bones are removed from the chops before cooking.

American Apple Balls, for recipe see page 35

Crunchy Chicken Casserole

Cooking time: 30 minutes
Oven: gas mark 8, 450°F
Dish: ovenproof casserole
Serves: 4

4 cooked chicken joints
10 oz. can condensed chicken soup
2 sticks celery, diced
2 oz. walnuts, chopped
½ small onion, chopped finely
4 tablespoons mayonnaise
1 tablespoon lemon juice
salt and pepper
2 eggs, hard-boiled and chopped
2 1-oz. packets potato crisps, crushed

Mix together all ingredients except the potato crisps. Place in a covered casserole and bake for 20 minutes. Remove lid, cover with crushed potato crisps and brown in the oven.

Handy hint: serve hot with a tossed green salad.

Chicken Napoli

Cooking time: 40 minutes
Dish: flameproof casserole
Serves: 4
Colour picture. page 21

1 oz. butter
2 tablespoons olive oil
4 chicken joints
1 medium onion, chopped finely
2 oz. bacon *or* ham, diced
8 oz. can tomatoes
4 oz. mushrooms, cut into quarters
4 tablespoons white wine *or* cider
1 small green pepper, de-seeded and cut into strips
8 oz. spaghetti

Melt the butter and oil in a large flameproof casserole and fry the chicken gently for about 20 minutes. When cooked, remove and keep hot. Add the onion to the dish and fry gently until soft, add the bacon, tomatoes, mushrooms and wine. Return the chicken to the dish and continue cooking slowly for 15 minutes, add the green pepper and cook for a further 5 minutes. Meanwhile, cook spaghetti in boiling salted water. Drain. Serve chicken joints arranged on spaghetti.

Handy hint: alternatively serve on hot rice. To prevent colouring the sauce grey, do not slice mushrooms but cut into quarters.

Chicken and Ham Pie

Cooking time: 25 minutes
Oven: gas mark 7, 425°F
Tin: baking sheet
Serves: 4

½ oz. margarine *or* butter
1 small onion, chopped finely
1 level teaspoon flour
5 tablespoons chicken stock
6 oz. chicken, cooked and diced
2 oz. ham, cooked and diced
2 teaspoons parsley, chopped
salt and pepper
13 oz. frozen puff pastry, thawed
milk *to glaze*

Melt the margarine and cook the onion gently until soft. Add the flour and cook for 2 minutes. Gradually add the chicken stock, stir until boiling and simmer for 3 minutes. Add the chicken, ham, seasoning to taste, and then cool. Roll out the pastry into two 8-inch circles. Place one circle on the baking sheet, put on the filling to within 1 inch of the edge. Damp the edge, cover with the second circle and seal firmly. With the back of the knife, make large scallops around the edge. Brush the pie with milk, make a small slit in the centre and decorate with some 'leaves' made from the pastry trimmings.

Handy hint: to roll two perfect circles, divide the pastry in half and shape each into a ball. Roll each forwards and backwards only, giving it a quarter turn before rolling again.

Pineapple Rolls

Cooking time: 20 minutes
Oven: gas mark 7, 425°F
Tin: baking sheet
Makes: 9

4 oz. short crust pastry (or
    7½ oz. frozen, thawed)
15 oz. can pineapple rings,
    drained

7 glacé cherries
2 tablespoons castor sugar
½ level teaspoon ground
    ginger
} mixed

Roll out pastry to a 12-inch square; using a 3-inch fluted cutter, cut out sixteen circles. Re-roll remainder of pastry and cut out a further two circles. Place nine of these on a baking sheet. Put a pineapple ring on each with a cherry in the centre; sprinkle with half the combined sugar and ginger. Cover with remaining pastry circles, brush with water and sprinkle with rest of the ginger and sugar. Bake in the centre of oven. Serve hot or cold with cream.

Handy hint: the circles of pastry will not be perfect shapes if the pastry cutter is twisted while cutting.

American Apple Balls

Cooking time: 45 minutes
Oven: gas mark 6, 400°F
Dish: deep ovenproof dish
Serves: 4
Colour picture, page 32

4 oz. short crust pastry (or
    7½ oz. frozen, thawed)
4 medium cooking apples

2 oz. sugar
1 oz. honey
redcurrant jelly

Roll the pastry to a long, narrow shape and cut into strips ½ inch wide. Peel and core the apples. Wrap each apple in slightly overlapping strips of pastry, starting at the top of the apple. Place on the dish and fill each centre with a teaspoon of redcurrant jelly. Put peelings, core, half pint water, sugar and honey in a pan and stew until syrupy. Strain the liquid and flavour with a little lemon juice. Pour the syrup over the pastry-covered apples and bake immediately. Baste frequently during cooking and serve in the ovenproof dish with the remaining syrup.

Handy hint: these apple balls will look particularly attractive if the strips are cut with a pastry wheel.

Raspberry and Apple Crumble

Cooking time: 30 minutes
Oven: gas mark 5, 375°F
Dish: 8-inch pie dish
Serves: 5–6

8 oz. fresh or frozen raspberries
2 large cooking apples, peeled,
    cored and sliced
1–3 oz. sugar

4 oz. flour
2 oz. sugar
2 oz. butter *or* margarine
1 teaspoon mixed spice
} crumble

Place raspberries and prepared apples in layers in pie dish, sprinkle each layer with sugar. Make a crumble mixture by mixing flour and 2 oz. sugar in a basin, then rub in fat, and stir in mixed spice. Spoon crumble mixture over fruit. Bake until golden.

Handy hint: serve hot or cold with custard or cream. Crumble mixture can be made in large quantities and frozen, to use when required.

Golden Grilled Sponge

Cooking time: 5 minutes
Dish: round platter
Serves: 6

1 oz. butter
1 oz. demerara sugar
1 oz. walnuts, chopped

9 oz. can pineapple chunks,
   drained and chopped finely
1 frozen cream sponge, unthawed

Mix butter and sugar together, stir in nuts and pineapple. Spread mixture on to top of frozen cream sponge and place cake under a hot grill. Grill approximately 5 minutes, until top browns lightly. Allow to thaw completely before serving as a cake or dessert.

Handy hint: chopped nuts are easier to prepare in an 'auto-chop' gadget.

Jiffy Cheesecake

Cooking time: 18 minutes
Time to set
Oven: gas mark 7, 425°F
Dish: 8-inch flan ring
Serves: 4–6

4 oz. short crust pastry (or
   $7\frac{1}{2}$ oz. frozen, thawed)
large can condensed milk
3 oz. lemon juice

8 oz. cream cheese, softened
whipped cream and ground
   nutmeg *to decorate*

Roll out the pastry and use to line the flan ring. Cover the pastry with greaseproof paper and scatter with uncooked rice or dried beans. Bake 'blind' in this way for 10 minutes, remove the greaseproof paper and rice or beans, and return to the oven for a further 5–8 minutes or until cooked. Remove flan ring and cool. Place the condensed milk in a basin and stir in the lemon juice and cream cheese. Mix well and put into flan case. Leave to set in a cool place. When set, decorate with whipped cream and ground nutmeg.

Handy hint: use smooth cream or curd cheese, *not* cottage cheese.

Cardinal Strawberries

Cooking time: nil
Dish: individual glass dishes
Serves: 3–4

8 oz. fresh strawberries, or
   frozen
8 oz. fresh raspberries, or frozen

2 oz. icing sugar, sifted
1 oz. almonds, blanched and
   chopped finely

Arrange strawberries in glass serving dishes. Sieve raspberries into a bowl and gradually beat in icing sugar. Spoon mixture over strawberries. Sprinkle with almonds and serve with whipped cream or ice cream.

Handy hint: blanch almonds by soaking in a little boiling water, then drain and squeeze out of their brown, papery skins.

Strawberry Tortoni

Cooking time: nil
Dish: sundae glasses
Serves: 4
Colour picture, page 56

8 oz. fresh strawberries, or frozen
   (reserve 4 for garnish)
1 oz. castor sugar
$\frac{1}{4}$ pint double cream

1 egg white, beaten stiffly
3 macaroons, crumbled coarsely
flavouring of kirsch *or* 1
   teaspoonful lemon juice

Sprinkle strawberries with sugar and put on one side. Whip the cream until thick and fold in the beaten white of egg. Fold in the kirsch or lemon juice, and the crushed strawberries. Finally add the crumbled macaroons. Divide between four dishes and top each with a whole strawberry. Serve immediately.

Handy hint: crush macaroons in a polythene bag, using a rolling pin.

EVENING OUT

Speed in the kitchen will be essential, whether you are eating before you go or when you get back; whether you're going to the pictures, to the theatre, late night shopping or just to evening classes.

There are times when all you need is something hot, nourishing and sustaining. But there are others when something a little more elaborate is required. In this section the ideas are for both those situations, and for meals either before you go or when you get home.

If you own an auto-timed oven—an invaluable aid to late meals—some of the recipes are specially for you: they involve 'automated' remote control cookery.

BEFORE YOU GO

Plaice Georgette

Cooking time: 1 hour 10 minutes
Oven: gas mark 6, 400°F
Dish: oval platter
Serves: 4 as first course
      2 as main course

2 large potatoes, scrubbed and pricked
8 oz. fresh or frozen plaice fillets
sauce
¼ pint milk
½ oz. butter
½ oz. flour
1 oz. cheese, grated
salt and pepper

½ oz. cheese, grated
1 tomato, skinned and halved (or sliced)
cooked peas

Bake the potatoes for 1 hour. Meanwhile, remove the dark skins from the fillets, roll them up and poach gently in the milk for 10 minutes. Remove fillets and reserve the liquor. Melt the butter in a pan, add the flour and blend in the fish liquor. Bring sauce to the boil, stirring. Add the cheese and seasoning. Cut the potatoes in half, and scoop out most of the pulp from each. Sieve the potato and mix with a little milk, then put in a piping bag. Place fish fillets in potato skins and pipe a border of potato around each. Pour a little cheese sauce over fish and sprinkle with grated cheese. Grill until the potato is browned and the cheese has melted. Serve with grilled tomato and peas.

Handy hint: to skin fillets, place skin-side down, work from tail end, gradually lift flesh from the skin, using the back of a knife.

Cod Portions with Mushrooms and Peanut Topping

Cooking time: 20 minutes
Dish: oval platter
Serves: 2

2 oz. margarine *or* butter
8 oz. frozen cod portions in breadcrumbs

2 oz. mushrooms, chopped coarsely
1 oz. salted peanuts, chopped
half a lemon

Melt the margarine or butter and fry the cod portions gently for 10 minutes, turning once. Remove from pan and keep hot. Add the mushrooms and peanuts to the pan and cook until the mushrooms are soft. Cut a slice of lemon and make two lemon butterflies; squeeze the juice from the remaining piece of lemon on the nuts and mushrooms in the pan. Place the cod portions on a serving dish and spoon the mushroom mixture over. Garnish with the lemon butterflies.

Handy hint: if the cod portions are cooked from frozen, be careful not to cook them too quickly, or the centre of each will still be raw when the crumb coating is golden brown.

Curry Meat Roll

Cooking time: 40 minutes
Oven: gas mark 6, 400°F
Dish: oval or rectangular platter
Serves: 5—6

12 oz. minced steak
4 tablespoons fresh white
   breadcrumbs
1 onion, chopped finely
2 oz. sultanas
1 egg, beaten lightly

2 teaspoons curry powder
salt and pepper
4 oz. short crust crust pastry (or
   7½ oz. frozen, thawed)
beaten egg or milk to glaze

Place the minced steak, breadcrumbs, onion and sultanas in a bowl, and mix well. Bind together with the beaten egg and add the curry powder and seasoning. Knead together and form into a roll about 10 inches long, on a floured board. Roll out the pastry into a rectangle measuring 12 × 10 inches, then damp the edges. Place the meat roll in the centre of the pastry and fold the pastry over it, sealing well. Place on a baking sheet with the join underneath. Make 3 small diagonal cuts in the top and decorate with pastry 'leaves'. Glaze with the beaten egg or milk, then bake.

Handy hint: cut into slices; serve hot or cold with a green salad.

Steaklet Casserole

Cooking time: 25 minutes
Dish: oval platter
Serves: 4

11 oz. frozen steaklets, thawed
1 oz. butter
2 medium onions, sliced
4 oz. mushrooms, sliced
4 rashers bacon, rind removed,
   chopped

14 oz. can tomatoes
2 teaspoons tomato purée
1 clove of garlic, crushed
salt
freshly ground pepper
boiled rice

Cut each steaklet into six squares and fry in a little butter for 8 minutes, turning frequently. Meanwhile, melt the rest of the butter in a saucepan and fry the onion until transparent, without browning. Add the mushrooms and bacon, then continue cooking for a further 3 minutes. Add the tomatoes, tomato purée, garlic and seasonings and cook for 2 minutes, finally add the cooked steaklets and leave to simmer over a gentle heat for 10 minutes. Serve with boiled rice.

Handy hint: garlic can be crushed either in a garlic press or beneath the blade of a heavy knife.

Beefburger Risotto

Cooking time: 40 minutes
Dish: oval entrée dish
Serves: 4

2 onions, chopped
4 oz. butter
8 oz. long grain rice
4 rashers bacon, chopped
¾ pint stock
salt and pepper
saffron (optional)

2 green apples, peeled, cored, diced
small can red peppers (pimientos),
   drained and sliced
4 oz. cooked peas
8 oz. frozen beefburgers, with or
   without onion, or 4 home-made
   hamburgers

Fry the onion gently in the butter for 5 minutes. Stir in the rice and bacon and cook for 2—3 minutes. Add the stock, bring to the boil, stir and season well, adding the saffron if available. Simmer until the stock has been absorbed (15—20 minutes). Add the apple, red peppers and peas, then cook for a further 5 minutes. Meanwhile, cook the beefburgers according to pack instructions, cut into quarters and serve with the rice. Garnish with parsley.

Handy hint: if saffron is not available, turmeric can be used to colour the rice. Use it sparingly; it has a very strong flavour.

Chicken in Cream Mushroom Sauce

Cooking time: 30 minutes
Dish: oval entrée dish
Serves: 2

1 oz. margarine *or* butter
2 chicken joints
4 oz. mushrooms, sliced

2 tablespoons cider
$\frac{1}{4}$ pint double cream
salt and pepper to taste

Melt the margarine or butter in a frying pan and fry the chicken gently for 25–30 minutes, turning once. Fry the mushroom slices during the last 5 minutes. Transfer the chicken to the serving dish and keep hot. Add the cider and cream to the pan. Stir well and simmer for 1 minute. Season to taste. Pour the sauce over the chicken and serve at once.

Handy hint: serve with a tossed green salad.

Cheese and Celery Flan

Cooking time: 30 minutes
Oven: gas mark 6, 400°F
      gas mark 4, 350°F
Tin: 7-inch flan ring
Serves: 4–5

4 oz. short crust pastry (or
   $7\frac{1}{2}$ oz. frozen, thawed)
1 head of celery, washed and diced
8 oz. cream cheese

1 teaspoon lemon juice
2 eggs
salt and pepper

Roll out pastry and line the flan ring. Line the pastry with greaseproof paper, cover the base with uncooked rice or dried beans and bake for 10 minutes. Remove from the oven. Lower the oven temperature. Boil the celery for 5 minutes in a little boiling salted water and drain. Put in a basin, add remaining ingredients and mix well. Pour into the flan case and return to the oven. Bake until set.

Handy hint: serve hot or cold, with a tossed green salad.

Pea, Cheese and Ham Supper Dish

Cooking time: 30 minutes
Dish: entrée dish
Serves: 3

4 oz. quick-cook macaroni
1 oz. butter *or* margarine
1 oz. flour
$\frac{1}{2}$ pint milk
4 oz. cheddar cheese, grated

salt and pepper
4 oz. cooked ham, cut $\frac{1}{2}$ inch
   thick, and cut into dice
8 oz. shelled peas (fresh *or*
   frozen)

Cook the macaroni as pack instructions. Drain and keep hot. Melt the butter in a saucepan, add the flour, cook gently without browning for 2–3 minutes, then gradually add the milk, stirring continuously. Cook for 3 minutes, add most of the cheese and season to taste. Meanwhile cook the peas and add them, with ham and macaroni, to the cheese sauce. Place in dish, sprinkle with remaining cheese and quickly grill for a minute.

Handy hint: cook the macaroni without a lid on the pan to prevent boiling over.

Strawberry Crunch

Cooking time: nil
Dish: individual tall glasses or
sundae glasses
Serves: 3

8 oz. fresh strawberries, or frozen,
   slightly thawed
4 chocolate digestive biscuits,
   crushed

5 oz. carton double cream,
   whipped

Layer the strawberries, biscuits and cream into sundae glasses, finish with a layer of cream and decorate with a strawberry.

Handy hint: put digestive biscuits into a polythene bag to crush with a rolling pin.

Tangy Apple Tart

Cooking time: 40 minutes
Oven: gas mark 6, 400°F
Tin: 7-inch flan ring
Serves: 4–6

4 oz. short crust pastry (or
   $7\frac{1}{2}$ oz. frozen, thawed)
1 oz. butter
2 oz. sugar
1 egg, beaten

1 teaspoon lemon rind, grated
1 tablespoon lemon juice
2 large cooking apples, peeled
   and grated coarsely

Roll out the pastry and line a 7-inch flan ring; reserve the pastry trimmings. Melt the butter, remove from the heat and add the remaining ingredients in the order given. Spoon the filling into the flan case. Cut the pastry trimmings into strips $\frac{1}{4}$-inch wide and make a lattice on top of the flan. Brush with a little milk and sprinkle with castor sugar. Bake. Serve warm or chilled.

Handy hint: be careful not to stretch the lattice strips as you place them on the flan or they will shrink back during cooking. To anchor securely, moisten ends and press gently at edge of flan.

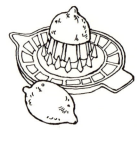

Orange Biscuit Flan

Cooking time: nil
Time to chill
Tin: 7-inch flan ring or
loose-bottomed cake tin
Serves: 5–6

2 oz. butter
8 oz. chocolate digestive
   biscuits, crushed
small can evaporated milk

$\frac{1}{2}$ oz. gelatine
4 tablespoons water
$6\frac{1}{4}$ fl. oz. can frozen concentrated
   orange juice, thawed

Melt the butter in a saucepan and add crushed biscuits. Mix well, then spread the mixture over bottom of tin. Place in a refrigerator to cool. Meanwhile, whisk the evaporated milk until it becomes thick and fluffy. Dissolve the gelatine in the water, then whisk into the milk gradually. Continue whisking and add the orange juice. When all the orange juice has been added, pour the filling into the flan case and leave to set in a refrigerator. Before serving, remove tin and decorate with either grated chocolate or chocolate buttons.

Handy hint: put the chocolate digestive biscuits in a polythene bag to crush with a rolling pin.

WHEN YOU GET BACK

Spinach Soup

Cooking time: 15 minutes
Dish: soup tureen or casserole
Serves: 5–6

1 oz. butter
1 oz. flour
½ pint milk
1 dessertspoon onion, grated
¾ pint chicken stock
12 oz. frozen spinach
salt, pepper and nutmeg
2 tablespoons cream

Melt the butter in a saucepan, add the flour then gradually add the milk, off the heat, stirring. Bring to the boil and cook for 2 minutes. Add the onion, chicken stock and spinach, then bring to the boil and cook for 8 minutes. Season.

Handy hint: reboil when you arrive home and, just before serving, stir in the cream.

Corn and Cod Chowder

Cooking time: 20 minutes
Dish: casserole or soup tureen
Serves: 4

4 4-oz. cod steaks
¼ pint water
¼ pint milk
6 oz. sweet corn, canned or frozen
1 medium onion, chopped
1 oz. butter
1 oz. flour
6 oz. can condensed mushroom soup
2 tomatoes, skinned and quartered
salt and pepper
parsley, chopped } for
croûtons of fried bread } garnish

Place the cod steaks, water, milk, sweet corn and onion in a large pan and bring to the boil. Simmer gently for 12–15 minutes until the fish is cooked. Lift out fish and drain. Melt the butter in a pan and stir in the flour. Blend in contents of other pan and bring to the boil, stirring. Add the canned soup and tomatoes and reheat, stirring. Flake the fish and return to the pan. Season well.

Handy hint: this may be prepared in advance and stored in a refrigerator. Later, reboil and garnish with parsley and croûtons.

Nancy's Fish Pie

Cooking time: 40 minutes
Oven: gas mark 7, 425°F
Dish: 2½–3-pint ovenproof dish
Serves: 6

1 lb. cod fillet
¾ pint milk
2 oz. margarine
4 sticks celery, chopped
2 oz. flour
4 oz. prawns *or* shrimps, prepared
salt and pepper to taste
7½ oz. frozen puff pastry, thawed
milk *to glaze*

Poach the fillets in the milk for 10 minutes. Meanwhile, melt the margarine in a saucepan and sauté the celery until soft but not brown, about 10 minutes. Add the flour and cook for 1 minute. Strain the milk into a measure and make up to 1 pint. Flake fish into fairly large pieces, removing the skin, and place in dish. Stir the milk into celery mixture and bring to the boil, stirring all the time. Add the prawns or shrimps and simmer for 5 minutes. Season well, pour over the fish and leave to cool. Roll out the pastry very thinly to a rectangle and cut out a cover for the pie, making sure that it is ½ inch wider on all sides than the dish. Damp the edges of the dish and carefully lay the pastry cover on top. Decorate edges and make a slit in the centre. Brush with a little milk. Bake until the pastry is golden brown. Serve hot.

Handy hint: reheat the pie at the same temperature for 20 minutes.

Baked Fish Charlotte

Cooking time: 40 minutes
Oven: gas mark 5, 375°F
Dish: greased, shallow oven-proof dish
Serves: 4

8 oz. plaice fillets
½ pint milk
2 eggs
1 tablespoon parsley, chopped

1 small onion, grated
salt and pepper
4 slices bread, crusts removed, buttered, cut into fingers

This recipe can be cooked in an auto-timed oven. Poach the fillets in the milk for 10–12 minutes until cooked. Drain, reserving the liquor, then skin and flake the fish. Meanwhile, beat the eggs together in a bowl, add the parsley, onion, salt and pepper, fish liquor made up to ½ pint, and the fish. Pour into the dish. Place the lightly buttered bread fingers over the fish mixture. Put the dish in a roasting tin half filled with water, and bake until the custard is set.

Handy hint: this could be auto-timed, allowing time for oven to heat, in addition to cooking time. Serve with colourful vegetables.

Frikadeller Croûte

Cooking time: 10 minutes then 45 minutes
Oven: gas mark 8, 450°F then gas mark 4, 350°F
Dish: oval platter
Serves: 4

1 medium onion, chopped finely
8 oz. minced beef
2 oz. bacon, rind removed, chopped finely
1–2 teaspoons tomato purée

¼ teaspoon garlic salt
salt and pepper to taste
7½ oz. frozen puff pastry, thawed
milk *or* beaten egg *to glaze*

Mix the onion, beef, bacon and seasonings together and form into a 'sausage' 10 inches long. Roll out the pastry very thinly to an oblong and trim to measure 12 × 8 inches. Damp the edges, then lay the meat mixture in the centre of the pastry. Seal all the edges carefully, then place the roll on a baking sheet with the joined edge underneath. Glaze with the milk or beaten egg, and make six diagonal slits in the top of the pastry. Roll out pastry trimmings, shape into 'leaves' and use for decoration. Bake in a hot oven before reducing the heat to complete cooking.

Handy hint: serve hot with gravy. Reheat at 350°F, gas mark 4, for 20 minutes.

Steaklet Kebabs

Cooking time: 15 minutes
Dish: oval platter
Serves: 2

5½ oz. frozen steaklets
4 rashers streaky bacon, rind removed, cut in half, rolled
4 tomatoes, halved
4 button mushrooms
2 oz. butter, melted

salt and pepper
6 oz. long grain rice
tomato sauce
8 oz. can tomatoes
salt and pepper
pinch of sugar

Cut each steaklet into four and arrange ingredients on four skewers in the following order: bacon roll, tomato, steaklet, mushroom, steaklet, tomato, bacon roll. Brush with melted fat, season and wrap in foil. Keep in a cool place. When you get home, grill the kebabs gently for 10–15 minutes turning them frequently. Cook rice in boiling salted water for about 15 minutes, drain in a sieve. Empty the can of tomatoes into a saucepan, bring to the boil and simmer for 10 minutes. Add seasoning and a pinch of sugar. Serve the kebabs on a bed of rice and hand sauce separately.

Handy hint: if using a spit-roaster, you can assemble kebabs on the skewers before you go out, wrap in foil and place in refrigerator.

Coq au Vin

Cooking time: 1 hour
Oven: gas mark 3, 325°F
Dish: large flameproof casserole
Serves: 4

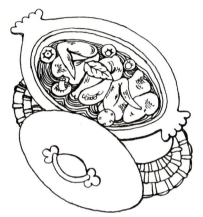

1 oz. butter
1 tablespoon olive oil
6 oz. button onions
4 oz. bacon, cut into strips
4 chicken joints
5 tablespoons brandy
1 oz. flour
¾ pint red wine
½ pint stock
4 oz. button mushrooms
1 bay leaf
1 teaspoon sugar
salt, freshly ground black pepper
fried croûtons, *for garnish*

This recipe can be cooked in an auto-timed oven. Melt the butter in a flameproof casserole, add the oil and cook the onions with the bacon until they are golden brown. Remove, and keep on a plate. Fry the chicken until slightly browned on both sides, add the brandy and set alight. When flame dies down, remove the chicken, add the flour to the pan and cook for 2 minutes. Gradually add the red wine and stock, stirring all the time. Replace the chicken, with the onions and bacon. Add the mushrooms, bay leaf, sugar and seasonings, then place the covered casserole in the oven for 30 minutes. Serve garnished with heart-shaped croûtons round the dish.

Handy hint: reheat at 325°F; the liquid must boil for at least 5 minutes.

Pizza Quickie

Cooking time: 25 minutes
Oven: gas mark 7, 425°F
Dish: round platter
Serves: 4–6

2 rashers lean bacon, rind removed, chopped
1 oz. butter
2 oz. mushrooms, sliced
1 large eating apple, peeled, cored and chopped
4 oz. short crust pastry (or 7½ oz. frozen, thawed)
8 oz. can tomatoes, drained
4 oz. cheese, grated
6 anchovy fillets, halved lengthwise

Fry bacon, mushrooms and apple until soft. Roll pastry to an 8-inch circle and place on baking sheet. Pull up edges to form a scalloped border. Spread tomatoes over pastry. Mix cheese and fried mixture together, then place on top of tomatoes. Arrange anchovy fillets in lattice design over pizza. Bake for 20 minutes.

Handy hint: to keep pastry shape, roll circle as advised on page 34.

Savoury Corn Flan

Cooking time: 40 minutes
Oven: gas mark 6, 400°F
Tin: 7-inch flan ring
Serves: 5–6

6 oz. sweet corn, canned or frozen
4 oz. short crust pastry (or 7½ oz. frozen, thawed)
1 oz. butter
½ oz. flour
¼ pint milk
1 egg
8 oz. can pink *or* red salmon
salt and pepper
2 small tomatoes, skinned

Cook the sweet corn as pack instructions. Roll out the pastry and line the flan ring. Melt the butter in a pan, remove from the heat and stir in the flour. Blend in the milk, return to the heat and bring to the boil, stirring. Cook for 2 minutes, remove from the heat and beat in the egg. Stir in the salmon and corn, mix well. Season. Put in flan case, arrange tomato slices on top and bake for 20–25 minutes.

Handy hint: serve cold with a tossed green salad.

Brandied Peaches

Cooking time: nil
Time to chill: 2 hours
Dish: glass fruit bowl
Serves: 6

6 large fresh peach halves *or*
  canned white peaches
2–3 fl. oz. brandy

6 fl. oz. double cream
2 oz. icing sugar
8 oz. fresh strawberries, or frozen

Arrange the peach halves in the serving dish and pour brandy over fruit. Cover dish and refrigerate for 2 hours. In a bowl, combine the double cream, icing sugar and crushed strawberries. Cover dish and refrigerate for 2 hours. Beat the sauce mixture until stiff, and serve with the fruit.

Handy hint: have fruit and sauce mixture in separate bowls. On your return, quickly whip sauce and serve.

Orange Cream Crunch

Cooking time: nil
Time to chill: 2–3 hours
Dish: 2–2½-pint glass serving dish
Serves: 4

small can condensed milk
juice of half lemon
¼ pint double cream, whipped
2 eggs, separated

½ can frozen concentrated orange
  juice, thawed
2 oz. butter, melted
2 oz. cornflakes, crushed
2 oz. castor sugar

Pour the condensed milk into a bowl and stir in lemon juice. Fold in whipped cream, egg yolks and orange juice. Whisk egg whites until very stiff, fold carefully into mixture. Pour into dish and leave to set. Mix butter, cornflakes and sugar together; put on top of orange cream. Leave in a cool place for 2–3 hours before serving.

Handy hint: put cornflakes in a polythene bag to crush.

Orange Soufflé

Cooking time: 15 minutes
Time to set
Dish: 5-inch soufflé dish or
4 × 3-inch soufflé dishes
Serves: 4

3 large eggs, separated
2 oz. castor sugar
1 oz. icing sugar, sieved
½ oz. gelatine
4 tablespoons water

½ can frozen concentrated orange
  juice, thawed
¼ pint double cream, whipped
whipped cream, angelica *or*
  pistachio nuts *to decorate*

Place the egg yolks and castor sugar in a large basin and whisk over a pan of hot water until thick and creamy. Stir in the icing sugar. Dissolve the gelatine in the water in a basin over a pan of hot water, then fold into egg and sugar mixture. Add the orange juice and stir well, fold in the whipped cream. Whisk the egg whites and fold in. Pour into the prepared dish, or dishes, and leave to set. When set, remove the 'collars' and decorate with whipped cream and angelica or pistachio nuts.

Handy hint: make collars for soufflé dishes by surrounding with a double foil band, standing 3 inches above top of the dish.

BE PREPARED FOR YOUR GUESTS

The main reason for inviting people to a meal or for the weekend is to enjoy their company! So plan menus to allow you to spend the maximum time with your guests and the shortest possible time in the kitchen. This is particularly important when several days of entertaining are involved. There is no fun in collapsing, exhausted, at the end of the visit.

If you own a freezer, entertaining can be very simple. Dishes can be prepared well in advance, if necessary, and components of meals can be stored until you want to complete the dishes.

In anticipating a visit, most hostesses will spend a few happy hours browsing through books and magazines for new ideas. Remember, exotic looking dishes need not require great skill and ingenuity. It is a good plan to choose at least one cold dish for each meal and concentrate your efforts on the hot one. Try to vary colours, textures, flavours and richness when planning your menu. And be sure to find out your guests' preferences and allergies, so that you can take them into account.

Most of the recipes in this section can be made completely or partially in advance, and there are some for special occasions like Christmas and Easter.

COOK-AHEAD MEALS

Cream of Broccoli Soup

Cooking time : 20 minutes
Dish: soup tureen or casserole
Serves: 3

1 pint chicken stock
9 oz. frozen broccoli
1 oz. margarine
2 level teaspoons onion, grated
1 oz. flour
1 pint milk
¼ pint single cream
salt and pepper

Bring the stock to the boil and cook the broccoli in it until tender (approximately 10 minutes). Pass contents of the pan through a nylon sieve, or liquidise. Melt the margarine and sauté the onion until soft, but not browned. Add the flour to form a roux, cook for 3—4 minutes. Blend in the milk, stir continuously until boiling, then simmer for 3—4 minutes. Add the sauce to the purée and reheat. Finally, stir in the cream and season to taste.

Handy hint: be careful not to brown the onion as it will destroy the attractive green colour of the broccoli.

Kipper Paste

Cooking time: 12 minutes
Dish: ramekin dishes
Serves: 4

6 oz. kipper fillets
1½ oz. butter, softened
freshly ground pepper and nutmeg to taste

Cook the fillets for 5 minutes, then carefully turn on to a plate. Remove the skin from the fish, then put fish and liquor through a fine mincer, or liquidise. Mix the minced kipper into the butter and season with pepper and nutmeg. Beat well until smooth and creamy. If put into small pots and covered loosely with foil, or with a layer of melted butter, the paste may be kept for 3 days in the refrigerator. Serve cold with toast.

Handy hint: this makes a tasty 'starter', or a sandwich filling.

Fish in Mushroom Scallops

Cooking time: 20 minutes
Dish: individual scallop shells or
glass dishes
Serves: 8

6 4-oz. fresh or frozen
  cod steaks
10 oz. condensed mushroom soup
1 teaspoon sherry, white wine *or*
  cider

pinch of garlic salt
1 (5—6 serving) packet instant
  potato
paprika *for garnish*

Poach the fish in a little water for 10 minutes. When cooked, drain, reserving liquor. Cut each steak into eight cubes. Divide the fish between eight scallop shells. Pour the soup into a pan, add two tablespoons of fish liquor, the sherry and garlic salt. Bring to the boil. Pour a little of this mushroom sauce over fish in each shell. Meanwhile, make up the instant potato and using a star nozzle and piping bag, pipe a potato border around the fish in each shell. Garnish with a little paprika sprinkled on the potato.

Handy hint: make the instant potato a little stiffer than usual for piping. To make richer, use an egg yolk and a little cream to mix.

Haddock and Prawn Salad

Cooking time: 15 minutes
Dish: round or oval platter
Serves: 4

12 oz. fresh or frozen
  fillet haddock
4 oz. prawns, peeled
4 inches cucumber, peeled and
  diced

$\frac{1}{4}$ pint mayonnaise
1 desertspoon parsley, chopped
lettuce

Poach the fillets in a little water for 10—15 minutes. When cooked, remove skin, flake and allow to cool. Add the prawns and cucumber to the cooled fish, then mix in the mayonnaise and parsley. Serve on a bed of lettuce.

Handy hint: if home-made mayonnaise is not available, add 2 tablespoons whipped cream to bottled mayonnaise. This will diminish the acid flavour.

Plaice Natasha

Cooking time: 20 minutes
Oven: gas mark 5, 375°F
Dish: ovenproof entrée dish
Serves: 3

3 large plaice fillets

stuffing
4 oz. soft herring roes
2 oz. breadcrumbs
1 level teaspoon parsley, chopped
little onion, grated
salt and pepper

sauce
1 oz. margarine
1 oz. flour
$\frac{1}{2}$ pint milk
3 tablespoons dry white wine
2 tablespoons single cream
2 oz. prawns, peeled
salt and pepper

Skin the fillets. Mix all the stuffing ingredients together and divide equally among fillets. Fold each fillet in half and place in the greased dish. Cover and bake. When cooked, lift on to a serving dish and keep hot; reserve the fish liquor. Melt the margarine in a small pan, add the flour and cook for 2 minutes. Gradually add the milk, the fish liquor and wine, then bring to the boil, stirring. Simmer for 3 minutes, then add the cream, off the heat. Lastly, add the prawns with seasoning to taste, and pour the sauce over the fish. Serve at once.

Handy hint: if it is necessary to reheat a sauce after adding cream, this should be done gently, for a short time.

Savoury Galette

Cooking time: 1 hour
Oven: gas mark 7, 425°F
Dish: oblong platter
Serves: 4–6

½ oz. dripping *or* cooking fat
2–3 medium onions, chopped finely
1 lb. minced beef
1–2 rounded teaspoons tomato
    purée
salt and pepper to taste

½ tablespoon parsley, chopped
½ pint beef stock
1 tablespoon cornflour
13 oz. frozen puff pastry, thawed
milk *or* beaten egg *to glaze*

Melt the fat in a medium sized saucepan and gently fry the onion for 5 minutes. Add the minced beef and continue cooking for a further 5 minutes, stirring continuously. Add the purée, seasoning, parsley and the stock, then bring to the boil. Cover the pan and simmer for 25 minutes. Blend the cornflour with a little cold water, add to the meat and continue cooking for a further 5 minutes, stirring. Remove from the heat and allow to become cold. Roll out the pastry very thinly to an oblong measuring 14 × 10½ inches and cut in two lengthwise, making one strip 14 × 5 inches and the second 14 × 5½ inches. Lay the narrower strip on a baking sheet and cover with the cold meat mixture to within 1 inch of the edge. Damp edges and cover with the wider strip, sealing carefully. Make slits across the top of the galette and if desired, decorate with pastry 'leaves' made from any trimmings. Glaze pastry and bake for 20 minutes. Serve hot, with a green vegetable.

Handy hint: this pastry will be thin when rolled out—lift on to baking sheet by rolling it round a rolling pin, to prevent stretching.

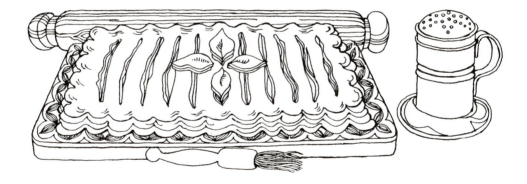

Filet de Porc Sauté Hongroise

Cooking time: 1 hour
Dish: oval platter
Serves: 3

1 oz. butter
1 lb. pork fillets, trimmed and cut
    into cubes
1 level dessertspoon paprika
1 rounded tablespoon flour
¼ pint chicken stock
2 fl. oz. sherry

½ green pepper, diced
5 oz. frozen small onions in white
    sauce
¼ pint water
2–3 oz. button mushrooms,
    sautéed in butter
2½ fl. oz. double cream

Melt the butter in a large frying pan, put in the cubes of pork and fry for 3–4 minutes. Stir in the paprika and flour, add the stock and sherry and bring to the boil. Simmer for 30–40 minutes. Add green pepper, onions and water and return to the boil, simmer for 3 minutes. Add the mushrooms and simmer for a further 3–4 minutes. Finally add the cream, adjust seasoning and serve immediately. Plain boiled rice could accompany this dish.

Handy hint: if it is necessary to reheat sauce after adding cream, this should be done gently, for a short time.

Smoked Haddock Jamboree

Cooking time: 20 minutes
Dish: ovenproof entrée dish
Serves: 4

8 oz. smoked haddock fillet
8 oz. shelled peas (or frozen)
sauce
1½ oz. butter
1½ oz. flour
¾ pint milk and fish liquor

8 oz. potatoes, cooked and diced
8 oz. tomatoes, skinned, de-seeded
   and cut into quarters
2 oz. prawns, peeled
salt and pepper
potato crisps, crushed

Poach the fish for 8–12 minutes, drain and reserve the liquor. Skin and flake the fish. Cook the peas. Top up fish liquor to ¾ pint with milk, and make the sauce. Add the fish, potatoes, tomatoes, and prawns. Season to taste. Place in the dish and sprinkle with the potato crisps. Reheat under a moderate grill, until the crisps turn golden brown.

Handy hint: to remove skins from tomatoes, immerse in boiling water for a few minutes; the skin splits and comes off easily.

Chicken Positano

Cooking time: 1 hour
Dish: oval platter
Serves: 4
Colour picture, page 61

2 oz. butter
4 chicken joints
1 medium onion, chopped finely
1 clove of garlic, crushed
4 oz. mushrooms, quartered
13 oz. can peeled tomatoes

¼ pint red wine
1 tablespoon cornflour
2 bay leaves
8 oz. long grain rice
1¼ pints chicken stock
1 tablespoon cornflour

Melt the butter and fry chicken on both sides for about 10 minutes; take out of pan and keep hot. Fry the onion and garlic without browning until soft. Add the mushrooms, replace chicken in the pan and add tomatoes, wine, sherry and bay leaves; cover and simmer very gently for 45 minutes. Meanwhile, cook the rice in the stock until liquid is absorbed, then put on serving dish. Remove chicken from pan and place on the rice. Mix the cornflour with a little water and add to contents of pan. Bring to the boil, stirring; cook for 3 minutes. Season carefully, then pour over chicken.

Handy hint: keep wine for cooking *cool*, in a screw-topped jar.

Chicken with Orange, Almond and Raisin Sauce

Cooking time: 50 minutes
Dish: large flameproof casserole
Serves: 4

1½ oz. butter
4 chicken joints
1 onion, chopped
1 oz. flour
pinch cinnamon
pinch ground ginger

½ can frozen concentrated orange
   juice, thawed
½ pint chicken stock
2 oz. almonds, blanched
2 oz. seedless raisins
salt and pepper

Melt the butter in a flameproof casserole and fry the chicken joints for 10 minutes, until lightly browned on both sides. Remove chicken, add the onion to pan and fry for 5 minutes. Remove pan from the heat and stir in the flour, cinnamon and ground ginger. Blend in the orange juice, and stock, then add the almonds and raisins. Return the pan to the heat and bring the sauce to the boil, stirring. Replace the chicken, cover pan and simmer gently for 30 minutes. Correct the seasoning and serve with boiled rice.

Handy hint: allow 1–2 tablespoons long grain rice per person, and boil in salted water for 10 minutes, without lid on the pan.

Raspberry Cheesecake, for recipe see page 51

Creamy Mustard Peas

Cooking time: 5 minutes
Serves: 4–6

1 lb. shelled peas (or frozen)
1 teaspoon dry mustard

4 tablespoons double cream

Cook the peas and drain. Put mustard in a basin and blend with a little cream. Stir in remainder of cream and pour into a pan. Add the peas and toss gently over low heat.

Bacon Dressed Peas

Cooking time: 5 minutes
Serves: 4–6

1 lb. shelled peas (or frozen)
2 oz. butter
1 tablespoon demerara sugar

3 rashers streaky bacon, rind
   removed and chopped
salt and pepper

Cook the peas and drain. Melt butter in a pan and add the demerara sugar. Stir until sugar has dissolved, then add the bacon. Cook gently for 3 minutes before tossing with the peas to reheat. Check the seasoning before serving.

Almond Green Beans

Cooking time: 7 minutes
Serves: 3

12 oz. green beans (or 8 oz. frozen)
1 oz. almonds

1 oz. butter
freshly ground black pepper

Cook the green beans and place in a serving dish. Meanwhile, skin the almonds and cut into shreds, put under a hot grill and brown lightly. Melt the butter in a pan, add the almonds, season with the ground pepper and pour over beans.

Florimon Sprouts

Cooking time: 10 minutes
Serves: 3

1 clove of garlic, cut in half
2 tablespoons lemon juice
2 tablespoons salad oil
pinch of paprika

pinch of pepper
$\frac{1}{4}$ level teaspoon salt
$\frac{1}{4}$ level teaspoon sugar
8 oz. prepared sprouts (or frozen)

Rub a small bowl with the cut clove of garlic. Blend the lemon juice, salad oil, seasonings and sugar together in the bowl. Cook the brussels sprouts and serve hot with the cold Florimon dressing.

Broccoli Polonaise

Cooking time: 8 minutes
Serves: 3

9 oz. frozen broccoli
1 egg, hard-boiled, chopped
$1\frac{1}{2}$ oz. butter

4 tablespoons fine white
   breadcrumbs

Cook the broccoli for 8 minutes, drain. Place in a serving dish. Sprinkle with the hard-boiled egg. Melt the butter and lightly brown the breadcrumbs, sprinkle over broccoli and egg and serve at once.

Broccoli Newport

Cooking time: 8 minutes
Serves: 3

9 oz. frozen broccoli
2 rashers bacon, rind removed
2 oz. butter

8 tablespoons breadcrumbs
1 egg, hard-boiled, chopped

Cook the broccoli for 8 minutes. Chop the bacon and fry until crisp, add butter and breadcrumbs. Fry until golden brown, mix with egg and serve on broccoli.

Orange Mallow Cream

Cooking time: nil
Time to freeze: 4 hours
Tin: ice tray
Serves: 3–4

6 oz. cream cheese, softened
8 oz. white marshmallows
¼ pint milk
½ 6¼ fl. oz. can frozen concentrated orange juice, thawed
¼ pint double cream, whipped

Whip the cream cheese until light and fluffy. Melt the marshmallows in the milk in a double saucepan. Allow to cool. Beat the marshmallow mixture into the cream cheese. Fold in the orange juice and lightly whipped cream. Freeze until almost set. Remove from the ice tray and beat. Pour back into ice tray and freeze for approximately 4 hours.

Handy hint: to serve, spoon into individual dishes and decorate with whipped cream and chopped nuts.

Raspberry Cheesecake

Cooking time: nil
Time to set
Tin: 8-inch greased, loose-bottomed cake tin
Dish: 10-inch round platter
Serves: 6
Colour picture, page 49

3 oz. butter
8 oz. digestive biscuits, crushed
2 oz. soft brown sugar
8 oz. fresh raspberries, or frozen, thawed
2 oz. icing sugar
8 oz. cream cheese
½ oz. gelatine
½ pint water
¼ pint double cream
1 teaspoon lemon juice

Melt the butter in a pan and add biscuit crumbs and sugar. Mix well, then press half the mixture into the cake tin. Reserve a few of the raspberries for decoration and sieve the remainder. Fold the icing sugar and cream cheese into the purée. Dissolve the gelatine in the water over a pan of hot water and allow to cool before adding to mixture. Whip the cream, reserve some for decoration, and fold the remainder into the raspberry mixture. Stir in the lemon juice, leave to thicken, stirring occasionally. Pour into the prepared tin, cover with a biscuit crust and leave to set. Turn out and decorate with cream and raspberries.

Handy hint: the raspberries could be liquidised rather than sieved.

Peach and Peanut Gâteau

Cooking time: 8 minutes
Dish: round flat plate
Serves: 6–8

1 cream and jam filled sandwich (fresh or frozen)
7¾ oz. can peach slices, drained and chopped (keep 4 slices *to decorate*)
2½ oz. unsalted peanuts, browned under grill
½ pint double cream, whipped

Place sponge on plate and remove top round. Add fruit to 1½ oz. peanuts and spread mixture over cream. Replace top round of sponge. Pipe cream in pyramids to cover top of sponge. Decorate with peach slices and remaining peanuts.

Handy hint: separate the two layers of sponge cake by lifting off the half without jam.

Chicken Waldorf Salad, for recipe see page 68

Christmas Ring, for recipe see page 62

Raspberry Delight

Cooking time: 5 minutes
Time to chill
Dish: round, shallow, ovenproof
Serves: 4

8 oz. fresh raspberries, or frozen
1 tablespoon sherry

3 oz. soft brown sugar
¼ pint double cream

Mix together raspberries, sherry and 1 oz. of sugar; place in serving dish. Whip cream until stiff and spread over the raspberries, covering completely. Chill in the refrigerator. Sprinkle 2 oz. of sugar over the top of the cream and place under a pre-heated grill until the sugar starts bubbling and browning. Return to refrigerator. Serve well chilled.

Handy hint: soft brown sugar melts more easily than demerara.

Black Bottom Pie

Cooking time: 15 minutes
Time to set
Oven: gas mark 6, 400°F
Tin: 7–8-inch flan ring
Dish: 10-inch round platter
Serves: 5–6

4 oz. short crust pastry (or
   7½ oz. frozen, thawed)
¾ pint milk
4 oz. sugar
1 oz. cornflour
1 egg, separated

¼ oz. gelatine
3 tablespoons water
3 oz. plain chocolate, melted
3 tablespoons undiluted frozen
   concentrated orange juice
¼ pint double cream, whipped

Roll out the pastry and line a pie plate or flan ring and bake 'blind'. Bake for 10 minutes, remove paper and beans and bake for a further 5 minutes. Cool. Blend a little milk with the cornflour and sugar, heat remaining milk in a saucepan and pour on to the blended mixture. Return to the saucepan and bring to the boil, stirring. Cook for 3 minutes, add the egg yolk and cool. Dissolve the gelatine in the water over a pan of hot water and add. Blend half the custard with the melted chocolate, and add the orange juice to remainder. Pour the chocolate custard into flan case and leave to set. Whisk the egg white and fold into the orange custard, pour into flan and leave to set. Decorate with whipped cream.

Handy hint: to bake blind, line the pastry with greaseproof paper and cover the base with a layer of uncooked rice or dried beans.

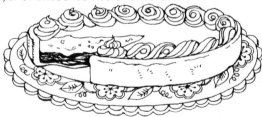

Gâteau Moya

Cooking time: nil
Dish: round flat platter
Serves: 6
Colour picture, page 24

1 cream and jam filled sandwich
   (fresh or frozen)
2 tablespoons apricot jam
4 level tablespoons almonds,
   flaked and toasted

11 oz. can mandarin oranges
¼ pint double cream
1 glacé cherry

Strain the syrup from the fruit. Heat the jam in a pan with a little of the mandarin juice. Spread a little of this round the side of the sponge, then coat with the chopped nuts. Arrange the mandarin oranges on the sponge, leaving ½-inch border round the edge. Place a glacé cherry in centre and brush the fruit with remainder of the jam glaze. Whip the cream until stiff and pipe round the edge of the sponge.

Handy hint: to coat the side of the sponge, put the flaked almonds on a sheet of greaseproof paper. Holding the cake on end, roll it in the nuts until side is evenly coated.

Turkey and Ham Slice

Cooking time: 25 minutes
Oven: gas mark 7, 425°F
Dish: platter
Serves: 6

1 oz. margarine
1 oz. flour
¼ pint milk
6 oz. turkey, cooked and diced
2 oz. ham, cooked and diced

1 tablespoon chopped parsley
salt and pepper to taste
13 oz. frozen puff pastry, thawed
milk *to glaze*

Melt the margarine, add the flour off the heat and gradually stir in the milk. Bring to the boil, stirring all the time. Simmer for 3 minutes, add the turkey, ham, parsley and season to taste. Roll out the pastry to an oblong measuring 14 × 10½ inches, and cut in two, lengthwise, making one strip 14 × 5 inches and the second 14 × 5½ inches. Place the narrower strip on a baking sheet, fill the centre with the turkey and ham, damp the edges with water. Fold the second piece of pastry in half lengthwise, and, leaving 1 inch border at the sides and top, make slits across the fold at ¼ inch intervals. Carefully open out the pastry and place over the filling, sealing the edges firmly. Brush with a little milk, then bake.

Handy hint: serve hot with a green salad.

Beef Wellington

Cooking time: 40 minutes
Oven: gas mark 7, 425°F
Dish: oval platter
Serves: 6–8
Colour picture, page 57

1 fillet of beef (2–2½ lb.)
2 oz. butter
4 oz. button mushrooms, sliced

1 tablespoon fresh mixed herbs, chopped
13 oz. frozen puff pastry, thawed
beaten egg *to glaze*

Trim and tie up the fillet. Melt the butter in a pan and quickly brown fillet on all sides. Remove from the pan and allow to cool. Sauté the mushrooms in the pan for a few minutes and add the herbs; drain and allow to cool. Roll the pastry out into a rectangle ⅛ inch thick. Mark the pastry lightly into three and cut off one-third. Spread the mushroom mixture on larger piece, place beef on top and press the pastry up round it. Damp edges of the other piece of pastry and place on top. Seal edges, brush with the egg glaze and decorate with 'leaves' made from pastry scraps. Place on a baking sheet and bake until well browned. Serve immediately, garnished with watercress.

Handy hint: this is delicious served with a mushroom and wine sauce. To make: add the grated rind and juice of 2 large oranges and 1 lemon to ¼ pint port wine and the juices from the cooked meat. Blend 1 level teaspoon arrowroot with a little of this, heat the rest, add a spoonful of arrowroot mixture; return to pan, bring to boil, stirring. Add ¼ teaspoon made-mustard, ½ teaspoon Worcestershire sauce, 2 oz. mushrooms, chopped finely. Simmer for 5 minutes.

Strawberry Tortoni, for recipe see page 36

Beef Wellington, for recipe see page 55

Almond Petits Pois

Cooking time: 3 minutes
Serves: 3–4

10 oz. frozen petits pois
½ oz. butter

1 oz. almonds, skinned and cut
    into shreds

Cook the petits pois for 3 minutes. Melt the butter, lightly brown the nuts and toss in the petits pois.

Festive Sprouts

Cooking time: 8 minutes
Serves: 3

8 oz. prepared sprouts (fresh or
    frozen)
1 oz. butter

2 oz. mushrooms, sliced
4 oz. chestnuts, boiled, skinned

Cook the sprouts for 8–10 minutes. Meanwhile, melt the butter and lightly fry the mushrooms until soft. Coarsely chop the chestnuts and toss with the mushrooms and sprouts.

Broccoli Mornay

Cooking time: 8 minutes
Serves: 3

9 oz. frozen broccoli
salt and pepper

3 tablespoons thick double cream
2 oz. cheese, grated

Cook the broccoli for 8 minutes. Place in an ovenproof dish, season well. Pour cream over top and sprinkle with cheese. Put under a hot grill until cheese has melted.

Corn and Cucumber

Cooking time: 5 minutes
Serves: 3

6 oz. sweet corn, canned or frozen
1½ oz. butter
½ tablespoon onion, grated

3 inches cucumber, diced
salt and pepper

Cook or heat the sweet corn. Meanwhile, melt butter and gently fry the onion for 2 minutes. Add cucumber and fry for 3 minutes before stirring in corn. Check seasoning.

Savoury Spinach

Cooking time: 5 minutes
Serves: 3–4

12 oz. frozen spinach
¼ oz. butter
1 small onion, chopped finely

⅛ pint single cream   } soured
1 teaspoon lemon juice } cream

Cook the spinach for 5–8 minutes, drain and return to pan. Meanwhile, melt the butter and fry the onion until soft but not browned. Add the onion to the spinach, mix well, pour in soured cream, return to the heat for a minute.

Beans à la Grecque

Cooking time: 25 minutes
Serves: 3

1 tablespoon olive oil
1 small onion, chopped finely
2 tablespoons tomato purée

½ teaspoon sugar
salt and pepper
8 oz. prepared whole French beans
    (or frozen)

Heat the olive oil and fry the onion gently for 3 minutes. Stir in the tomato purée, sugar, salt and pepper. Add the beans and cover pan. Simmer gently for 15–20 minutes until beans are cooked, stirring occasionally. Check seasoning and serve.

Orange Celebration Pudding

Cooking time: 15 minutes
Time to set: 2–3 hours
Dish: individual glass dishes
Serves: 4–6

2 oz. marshmallows
1 level teaspoon gelatine
1 oz. castor sugar
½ can frozen concentrated
  orange juice, thawed
4 oz. ginger nut biscuits, crushed

1 oz. walnuts, chopped
2 oz. raisins
2 oz. cut mixed peel
pinch of cinnamon
¼ pint double cream, lightly
  whipped

Place the marshmallows, gelatine, sugar, and orange juice in a sauce-pan and heat slowly, stirring, until the marshmallows have melted. Remove from heat and fold in the biscuits, walnuts, raisins, mixed peel and cinna-mon. Allow to cool slightly, then fold in the cream. Pour into a dish or small individual dishes and leave to set for about 2–3 hours before serving.

Handy hint: do not allow to boil while melting marshmallows, etc.

Chestnut Layer Gâteau

Cooking time: 15 minutes
Oven: gas mark 7, 425°F
Dish: round platter
Serves: 5–6

13 oz. frozen puff pastry, thawed
8 oz. can chestnut purée
½ pint double cream

2 oz. icing sugar
2 oz. plain chocolate, melted

Cut the pastry into three equal sections and roll each out thinly on a floured surface. Cut three 7-inch circles using a plate or saucepan lid as a guide. Transfer each in turn on to a baking sheet, prick gently with a fork, then bake. Cool. Meanwhile, place the purée, double cream and icing sugar in a bowl and whisk together until thick. Spoon this mixture into a piping bag with a star nozzle. Trim the pastry circles. Pipe the cream mixture on to one circle and place second on top. Pipe on to the top of the second circle. Spread the melted chocolate over the third circle; when cool, pipe a circle of cream mixture around the edge. Place this on top of gâteau and serve.

Handy hint: assemble no more than a couple of hours before eating.

Tangy Mincemeat Tarts

Cooking time: 10 minutes
Time to set
Dish: serving platter
Oven: gas mark 6, 400°F
Makes: 24–28

7 oz. short crust pastry (or
  13 oz. frozen, thawed)
half 14½ oz. jar mincemeat
small can condensed milk

4 oz. cream cheese
2 tablespoons lemon juice
grated lemon peel *to decorate*

Roll out the pastry on a floured surface and cut out as many 3-inch circles as possible. Use these to line patty tins; prick the pastry then bake. Remove pastry cases from tins and cool. Place a little mincemeat in the base of each. Meanwhile, mix together the condensed milk and cream cheese until smooth. Stir in the lemon juice. (The mixture will then begin to thicken.) Leave in a cool place until almost set. Pipe or spoon a little of the mixture on to each tart, covering the mincemeat. Decorate each with a little grated lemon peel and serve lightly chilled.

Handy hint: cut pastry without twisting the cutter. This ensures perfect circles and helps to prevent shrinking during baking.

Kipper Pizza, for recipe see page 67

Chicken Positano, for recipe see page 48

Christmas Amber

Cooking time:
flan: 15 minutes
meringue: 30 minutes
Oven:
flan: gas mark 6, 400°F
meringue: gas mark 4, 350°F
Dish: 7–8-inch pie dish
Serves: 4–5

1 lb. cooking apples
2 teaspoons water
juice of half a lemon
1 oz. sugar
½ oz. raisins, ½ oz. glacé cherries
juice of 1 orange *or* 2 tablespoons
   of cointreau
4 oz. short crust pastry (or
   7½ oz. frozen, thawed)

2 egg yolks
1 oz. sugar
grated rind of 1 orange
1 oz. flour
¼ pint milk
2 egg whites
4 oz. sugar

Peel and slice the apples and cook with the water, lemon juice and 1 oz. sugar until soft; allow to cool. Soak the raisins and cherries in the orange juice or cointreau. Roll out pastry and line the pie dish. Mix the yolks with 1 oz. sugar, add the grated orange rind, the flour and milk. Put in a small saucepan and cook over a low heat stirring all the time; add the apple pulp, glacé cherries and raisins, then pour into the lined pie dish. Bake. Meanwhile, whisk the egg whites until stiff, fold in the 4 oz. sugar, spread over the apple mixture. Sprinkle with a little castor sugar and return to cooler oven for 30 minutes until the meringue is set.

Handy hint: whisk egg whites until they stand in peaks. Continue whisking until bowl can be inverted without the whites falling out.

Christmas Ring

Cooking time: 20 minutes
Oven: gas mark 6, 400°F
Dish: round platter
Serves: 6–8
Colour picture, page 53

7½ oz. frozen puff pastry, thawed
filling
4 oz. ground almonds
4 oz. castor sugar
½ beaten egg
lemon juice to flavour

little beaten egg
to decorate
glacé icing
chopped glacé fruits
chopped or flaked nuts

Roll out the pastry to a strip approximately 5 × 20 inches. Mix the ground almonds, sugar, egg and lemon juice together. Form into a long sausage shape, the length of the pastry, and place down the centre of it. Damp the edges of the pastry and fold them over the almond mixture completely, to form a long roll. Press edges together gently and, with the wrap underneath, form into a circle, joining the two ends together neatly. Lift on to the baking sheet, brush over with beaten egg, then bake. Cool on a wire rack. When cold, pour over a thin glacé icing and sprinkle liberally with chopped glacé fruits and nuts.

Handy hint: serve warm. This is very good served with coffee.

Mincemeat Plait

Cooking time: 20 minutes
Oven: gas mark 7, 425°F
Dish: oblong platter or board
Serves: 6

8 oz. mincemeat
2 oz. glacé cherries, chopped
2 oz. almonds, blanched and
   chopped
13 oz. frozen puff pastry, thawed

beaten egg *to glaze*
4 oz. icing sugar   } icing
1 tablespoon lemon juice }
extra chopped cherries and
   blanched almonds *to decorate*

Combine the mincemeat, glacé cherries and almonds for the filling. Roll out pastry to an oblong, 12 inches wide and 14 inches long. Lightly mark the pastry into three, lengthwise. Brush the edges of the pastry with water. Make 3-inch cuts, 1 inch apart, diagonally along the edges of the pastry. Place the filling down the centre one-third and fold cut strips over, alternately, to give a plaited effect. Seal the ends. Place on a baking sheet, glaze and bake. Cool. Blend together the sifted icing sugar and lemon juice, adding a little boiling water if necessary to give a smooth glacé icing. Spoon over plait and sprinkle with chopped cherries and almonds.

Handy hint: try not to stretch pastry, to avoid it shrinking.

Easter Bonnet

Cooking time: nil
Dish: round platter
Serves: 5–6

14 oz. can cherries
1 teaspoon arrowroot
1 cream and jam filled sandwich
   (fresh or frozen)

3 tablespoons desiccated coconut,
   toasted

Drain syrup from the cherries and blend with arrowroot. Put in a pan and bring to the boil, stirring. Simmer for 3 minutes, then cool. Stone and chop the cherries, reserving eight for decoration. Remove the top of the sponge and using a 3–3½-inch cutter, cut a circle from the centre to represent the 'crown' of the bonnet. Return the outer circle to the sponge and pile the chopped cherries into the centre. Replace the 'crown'. Brush the top of the bonnet with the thickened syrup and dust with the coconut. Cut the reserved cherries in half, and place around the base of the 'crown'. Glaze cherries with syrup and decorate bonnet with ribbon.

Handy hint: cherry/olive stoners are sold by most large stores.

Orange and Gin Cup

Cooking time: nil
Makes: 3¼ pints

6¼ fl. oz. can frozen concentrated
   orange juice, thawed
½ pint gin

1 quart cider
mint leaves   } to
slices of cucumber } decorate

Make up the orange juice as directed on the can, add the gin and cider, mix well and serve chilled. Decorate with mint leaves and slices of cucumber.

Handy hint: if a punch bowl is not available, use a glass fruit bowl.

Sparkling Wine Punch

Cooking time: nil
Makes: 3½ pints

6¼ fl. oz. can frozen concentrated
   orange juice, thawed
1 pint medium sweet white wine

¼ pint sherry, 1 pint lemonade
strawberries, raspberries and slices
   of orange *to decorate*

Make up the orange juice as directed on the can and add the wine, sherry and lemonade. Chill and decorate with strawberries, raspberries and slices of orange.

Handy hint: slice orange with rind *thinly*: thick slices will sink.

CRISIS COOKERY

If this is really a crisis—turn straight to the recipes. But, if you have a moment, let me reassure you that there are some recipes for the unskilled, well-meaning husband and older children, and some for preparation in advance. Each section is clearly marked.

On the other hand, if you are just browsing, perhaps this is the moment to remember the value of a well stocked larder, frozen food compartment or freezer. In a crisis, there is no substitute for having everything to hand, and keeping a cool head.

RECIPES FOR THE UNSKILLED

Souper Sausages

Cooking time: 15 minutes
Dish: casserole or soup tureen
Serves: 4

6 oz. spaghetti
1 oz. butter
1 onion, chopped finely
12 oz. skinless pork sausages
sliced in ½-inch pieces

10 oz. can condensed tomato soup
few drops Worcestershire sauce
salt and pepper

Cook the spaghetti in boiling salted water for about 12–15 minutes, drain and keep warm in the serving dish. Meanwhile, melt the butter in a pan, add the onion and cook without browning, until transparent. Add the sausages and cook for a further 5 minutes. Stir in the soup and Worcestershire sauce, season well and heat through. Pour the mixture over the spaghetti.

Handy hint: cook the spaghetti without a lid on the pan and, to add gloss, stir in a knob of butter after draining.

Crispy Deckers

Cooking time: 20 minutes
Oven: gas mark 7, 425°F
Dish: oval platter
Serves: 2

4 large slices of bread
little margarine

4 oz. frozen beefburgers *or*
2 home-made hamburgers

From each slice of bread cut a circle, the same size as the beefburgers, and spread one side of each very lightly with margarine. Place two circles, fat side down, on a baking sheet and put a beefburger on each, then top with the remaining rounds. Bake and serve hot.

Handy hint: serve with mustard or horseradish sauce, and a salad.

Corn and Tuna Salad

Cooking time: 5 minutes
Dish: salad bowl or platter
Serves: 3–4

6 oz. sweet corn, canned or frozen
1 large carrot, grated
1 small green pepper, de-seeded
 and chopped finely
8 oz. can tuna, flaked
1 tablespoon mayonnaise

1 teaspoon lemon juice
salt and pepper
1 small lettuce
lemon wedges
parsley } for garnish

Cook or heat the corn for 5 minutes. Drain and cool. Mix together the carrot, green pepper and tuna, and then add the sweet corn, mayonnaise and lemon juice. Season. Line the dish with lettuce leaves and pile the salad in the centre. Garnish and serve.

Handy hint: over-cooking toughens sweet corn.

Quick Steaklet Stroganoff

Cooking time: 25 minutes
Dish: oval entrée dish
Serves: 3–4

$1\frac{1}{2}$ oz. butter
1 medium onion, sliced thinly
6 oz. long grain rice
11 oz. frozen steaklets, cut into
 $\frac{1}{4}$-inch strips

6 oz. can condensed mushroom
 soup
half soup-can of water
1 teaspoon tomato purée
salt, freshly ground pepper

Melt the butter in a pan and fry the onion without browning, until transparent. Meanwhile, boil the rice, without the lid on the pan. Add the strips of steaklet and fry quickly until lightly browned. Stir in the mushroom soup, water, tomato purée and seasonings. Simmer for 8 minutes and serve on the cooked rice.

Handy hint: tomato ketchup may be used instead of purée, if liked.

Chocolate Mousse Parfait

Cooking time: nil
Dish: individual sundae glass
Serves: 1

small frozen chocolate mousse,
 cut into cubes
1 macaroon, crumbled

1 pear, peeled, cored and diced
chocolate sauce
chopped nuts

Mix together the mousse cubes, macaroon and pear. Place in a glass dish, then pour over the chocolate sauce. Sprinkle with chopped nuts and serve. Chocolate sauce can be made easily by mixing one tablespoon of chocolate-spread with a little hot milk.

Handy hint: bought chocolate sauce could be used, if preferred.

Arctic Melba

Cooking time: nil
Time to thaw
Dish: glass dishes
Serves: 5

1 frozen *Arctic roll**
15 oz. can peach halves
2 tablespoons raspberry jam,
 sieved and thinned with water

chopped nuts
ice cream wafers, halved

*Registered Trade Mark

Cut the *Arctic roll* into five slices. Place in glass dishes and arrange a peach half on each slice. Spoon over the raspberry jam. Sprinkle with chopped nuts, and serve with ice cream wafers.

Handy hint: cut the *Arctic roll* while still frozen, and allow to thaw for about $\frac{1}{2}$ hour before serving.

Chocolate Banana Boats

Cooking time: nil
Dish: individual plates
Serves: 4

4 oz. plain chocolate
¼ pint hot water
2 level tablespoons castor sugar
2 oz. butter

4 chocolate éclairs, fresh or frozen
4 bananas
2 level tablespoons chopped nuts
wafer biscuits

Break the chocolate into pieces and place in a medium sized saucepan. Add the hot water and sugar, melt together over a low heat. Bring to the boil and allow to simmer until the sauce becomes syrupy. Remove from the heat and beat in the butter. Leave to cool. Cut the éclairs in half lengthwise, place each half on an individual plate, cream-side uppermost. Cut four bananas in half lengthwise and place along the éclairs, cut-side down. Pour sauce over each and sprinkle with chopped nuts. Place a wafer in the centre for a sail.

Handy hint: if using frozen, cut éclairs in half while still hard, using a sharp knife.

DISHES PREPARED IN ADVANCE

Kipper Pizza

Cooking time: 40 minutes
Oven: gas mark, 7, 425°F
Dish: large round platter
Serves: 6
Colour picture, page 60

6 oz. kipper fillets
8 oz. self-raising flour ⎫ scone
2 oz. butter ⎬ dough
¼ pint milk ⎭
salt
2 tomatoes, skinned, de-seeded
  and chopped

½ onion, chopped finely
pinch mixed herbs
salt and pepper
2 oz. cheese, grated
2 rashers bacon, halved lengthwise
parsley, chopped

Cook the fillets for 5 minutes, drain and add a knob of butter. Make up the scone dough by rubbing in the flour and butter, then mixing together with the milk. Knead lightly and press into a round, 12 inches in diameter, on a greased baking sheet. Press up rim. Bake for 15 minutes. Remove from oven and arrange tomato and onion on dough, sprinkle with herbs and seasoning. Flake the kipper fillets and spread over the mixture. Sprinkle with cheese and criss-cross the bacon strips on top. Bake again until brown. Sprinkle with parsley to serve.

Handy hint: spread the mixture to within 1 inch of the edge of the dough to prevent cheese running off when it melts.

Beefburger Pasties

Cooking time: 20–25 minutes
Oven: gas mark 7, 425°F
Dish: large oval platter
Serves: 4

13 oz. frozen puff pastry, thawed
8 oz. frozen beefburgers *or*
  4 home-made hamburgers

4 teaspoons horseradish sauce
1 tomato, sliced
beaten egg

Roll out pastry thinly and cut into eight circles (4-inch diameter). Place four circles on baking sheet and top each with a beefburger. Spread with horseradish sauce and place one slice of tomato on each. Brush pastry edges with water and cover with remaining circles. 'Knock-up' and 'flute' edges, then brush with beaten egg. Bake.

Handy hint: cut round a small saucer to make pastry circles.

Russian Chicken Pie

Cooking time: 30 minutes
Oven: gas mark 8, 450°F
Dish: large flat platter or board
Serves: 4—5

1 oz. butter
1 oz. flour
¼ pint chicken stock
¼ pint milk
salt and pepper

6 oz. chicken meat, cooked, diced
13 oz. frozen puff pastry, thawed
1 egg, hard-boiled, sliced
egg *or* milk *to glaze*

Melt the butter in a pan, add the flour, remove from the heat and gradually add the stock and milk, stirring. Return to the heat, bring to the boil and cook for 2 minutes, stirring continuously. Season to taste. Cool, then add the cooked chicken. Roll out the pastry to a 14-inch square and place on a baking sheet. Place the filling in the centre and arrange the slices of egg over the filling. Damp the edges of the pastry and bring the four corners to the centre, forming an envelope. Seal edges well, brush with egg or milk, then bake until golden.

Handy hint: serve hot or cold with a tossed green salad.

Cod Steaks Mayonnaise

Cooking time: 15 minutes
Dish: individual salad dishes or scallop shells
Serves: 2

7 oz. frozen cod steaks
¼ pint mayonnaise
lettuce

for garnish
tomato, spring onions, watercress
and sliced radish

Poach the cod steaks in a little water for 10—15 minutes. When cooked, remove and allow to cool. Coat each steak with mayonnaise and serve on a bed of lettuce. Garnish with the remaining salad ingredients.

Handy hint: after cooking, drain the cod steaks on kitchen paper.

Chicken Waldorf Salad

Cooking time: 30 minutes
Dish: shallow dish or salad bowl
Serves: 3—4
Colour picture page 52

1½ oz. butter *or* 2 tablespoons oil
2 chicken joints
3 sticks celery, chopped roughly
1 medium red-skinned eating
   apple, cored and diced

1 oz. walnuts, chopped
4 tablespoons mayonnaise
salt and pepper
1 lettuce, washed
watercress and tomato *for garnish*

Heat butter or oil in a pan and fry chicken gently for about ½ hour. Drain and allow to cool. Remove the meat from the joints and cut into shreds. Mix meat with celery, apple and walnuts and fold in mayonnaise. Season well. Pile the salad on a bed of lettuce. Garnish with watercress and tomato.

Handy hint: leave the red skin on the apple as it looks very attractive in the salad.

Vegetable Slice

Cooking time: 25–30 minutes
Oven: gas mark 7, 425°F
Dish: large oval platter
Serves: 4–6

13 oz. frozen puff pastry, partially thawed
8 oz. frozen mixed vegetables
14 oz. can tomatoes, drained
1 clove of garlic, crushed
seasoning
2 oz. cheese, grated
egg, *to glaze*, optional

Roll out pastry to form an oblong 20 × 9 inches. Cut into two oblongs 10 × 9 inches. Trim edges and place one on baking sheet. On the other oblong, cut out *four* large diamonds across the centre, leaving a ¾-inch border all round. To uncooked mixed vegetables add tomatoes and garlic. Season and spread evenly over the pastry on baking sheet, within ½ inch of the edge. Sprinkle with cheese. Dampen edges of pastry and cover with second oblong. Seal edges, 'knock-up' and 'flute'. Brush with beaten egg, then bake.

Handy hint: to cut diamonds: fold pastry in half lengthways, and cut triangles to within ¾ inch of the edge.

Apple Strudel

Cooking time: 25–30 minutes
Oven: gas mark 7, 425°F
Dish: 17-inch long platter or board
Serves: 4–6

7½ oz. frozen puff pastry, thawed
1 oz. butter, melted

filling
2 large cooking apples, peeled, cored, thinly sliced
1 oz. currants, 1 oz. sultanas
2 oz. sugar
1 teaspoon mixed spice
3 plain biscuits, crushed

Roll out the pastry as thinly as possible—approximately 14 × 15 inches. Brush with melted butter. Mix filling ingredients together and sprinkle over the pastry. Roll up pastry and filling and seal the edges. Place on a baking sheet and bake. When cooked, dust lightly with icing sugar, and return to oven for a further 2–3 minutes to glaze. Serve warm or cold with cream.

Handy hint: prepare pastry first, to keep apples a good colour.

Orange Bread and Butter Pudding

Cooking time: 30 minutes
Oven: gas mark 5, 375°F
Dish: greased 2-pint pie dish
Serves: 5

butter
½ large loaf, crusts removed, cut into ¾-inch slices
2 oz. sultanas
1 pint milk
2 eggs
½ can frozen concentrated orange juice, thawed
2 oz. castor sugar

Butter the slices of bread well. Cut each slice into cubes and place these with the sultanas in the dish. Whisk the milk, eggs, orange juice and sugar lightly together, then pour over the bread. Cook in the oven until set. Serve hot or cold.

Handy hint: to prevent an egg mixture curdling, place dish in a tin half full of water to cook.

SLIMMING CLOCK-WATCHERS

Most people eat food they enjoy, regardless of any dietary considerations. No one really sits down to a plate of calcium, protein and vitamin C. It's the same on a slimming diet too. There's no reason why we shouldn't eat the food we enjoy—as long as we limit the total number of calories eaten—which means being careful about the amount of fat and carbohydrate in meals.

The simple fact is that if you want to lose weight, you must take in fewer calories. The reason why you gain weight in the first place is usually just that you eat more calories than you need for your particular energy requirements. Everyone uses up the food they eat at a different rate. This accounts for the annoying fact that some people can eat anything and remain slim, while others put on weight after the slightest indulgence.

Because it may seem disheartening to have to watch what you eat all your life, it's a big help to choose dishes that you're going to want to live with. They needn't be dull.

If you cook for a family, you may face an extra problem. They may not need to slim too! This need not mean you must either abstain yourself or starve the family! All the family will enjoy these recipes and by giving them a few extras they won't starve.

The approximate calorie content, per portion, has been calculated for each recipe. The table below will show you roughly how many calories you need each day.

Approximate daily calorie requirement

Man	Woman	Woman	Child	Child
	Adult	Pregnant/Lactating	3—5 years	12—15 years
2,600—3,600	2,000—2,500	2,400—2,700	1,600	2,300—2,800

Colour and taste play an important part in any diet, but particularly in a slimmer's diet. Try some of these recipes to satisfy an appetite without ruining a diet, and to tantalise the taste buds.

Bean and Cod Salad

Cooking time: 15 minutes
Time to chill
Dish: entrée dish
Serves: 4

Calories per portion: 140

1 lb. fresh or frozen cod fillet
12 oz. prepared sliced green beans
8 oz. tomatoes, skinned, quartered
   and de-seeded
5 oz. carton low fat natural
   yoghourt

1 small onion, grated
salt and pepper
$\frac{1}{4}$ teaspoon dry mustard
lemon and parsley *for garnish*

Poach the fish for 15—20 minutes in a little milk. Cut into cubes and allow to cool. Cook the beans for 2—3 minutes only, drain and refresh under cold water; mix with the tomatoes. Stir the yoghourt, onion and seasonings together, then mix with the fish. Place the beans and tomatoes round the edge of a serving dish and pile the fish in the centre. Serve chilled, garnished with lemon and parsley.

Handy hint: put the beans in a nylon or wire sieve to refresh them under cold water.

Fish Salad

Cooking time: 15 minutes
Dish: individual dish or
scallop shell
Serves: 1

Calories per portion: 200

4-oz. piece haddock fillet
1 tablespoon cucumber, diced
2 tablespoons mayonnaise
squeeze of lemon juice

watercress
1 tomato, skinned, quartered and
de-seeded

Poach the steak for 8–10 minutes in a little milk. Cool and flake, add the cucumber and mix in the mayonnaise and lemon juice. Arrange the watercress round the edge of a scallop shell or small dish. Pile the fish mixture in the centre and garnish with the tomato.

Handy hint: skin the tomato after dipping into boiling water for a few minutes.

Haddock Creole

Cooking time: 15 minutes
Dish: oval entrée dish
Serves: 4

Calories per portion: 80

1 lb. fresh *or* frozen haddock steaks
sauce
8 oz. can tomatoes
quarter green pepper, diced

1 tablespoon spring onions,
chopped
1 teaspoon Worcestershire sauce
salt and pepper

Poach haddock steaks for 10–15 minutes. Drain and keep hot on dish. Put all other ingredients in a liquidiser and blend to a smooth sauce. (If no liquidiser is available—chop thoroughly.) Heat sauce in a pan and pour over the steaks. Garnish with a little spring onion or green pepper.

Handy hint: for non-slimming members of the family, pipe mashed potato round the sides of the ovenproof dish. Grill until golden brown, before placing the fish in the centre.

Tangy Haddock Grill

Cooking time: 20 minutes
Dish: large oval platter
Serves: 3–4

Calories per portion: 140–190

13 oz. fresh or frozen
    haddock fillets
2 oz. cottage cheese

1 oz. butter
2 gherkins, chopped
salt and pepper

Grill the fillets for 5 minutes, skin-side uppermost, turn over and continue to grill for a further 5 minutes. Mix together all other ingredients and spread over the fillets. Return to grill and cook until the topping bubbles and begins to brown.

Handy hint: accompany this with a green salad. Non-slimmers could also have French bread.

Cod Steaks Provençale

Cooking time: 30 minutes
Time to marinate
Oven: gas mark 5, 375°F
Dish: ovenproof entrée dish
Serves: 4

Calories per portion: 135

14 oz. fresh or frozen cod steaks
½ pint dry white wine
1 medium onion, chopped

8 oz. can tomatoes
1 clove of garlic, crushed
freshly ground pepper, salt

Marinate the cod steaks in the wine for at least an hour. For the sauce, lightly fry the onion, add the tomatoes, garlic and seasoning. Strain the liquor from the fish and add to the sauce. Place cod steaks in the dish, pour over sauce. Bake for 25 minutes.

Handy hint: to prevent the cod steaks floating in the wine, cover closely with foil.

Cod and Vegetable Parcels

Cooking time: 25 minutes
Oven: gas mark 6, 400°F
Dish: entrée dish
Serves: 2

Calories per portion: 190

7 oz. fresh or frozen cod steaks
1 oz. button mushrooms, sliced
¼ bunch spring onions, chopped
  or ½ small onion, chopped finely

1 tablespoon lemon juice
salt and pepper
½ oz. butter
parsley and tomato *for garnish*

Cut two pieces of foil about 6 × 10 inches, place a cod steak on each, and pile the vegetables on top. Sprinkle with the lemon juice, season well and add a knob of butter. Fold over the foil to completely enclose the fish, place on a baking sheet and bake. When cooked, unwrap the parcels. Serve with the fish liquor poured over. Garnish with parsley and tomato.

Handy hint: this method of cooking is very good for conserving nutrients.

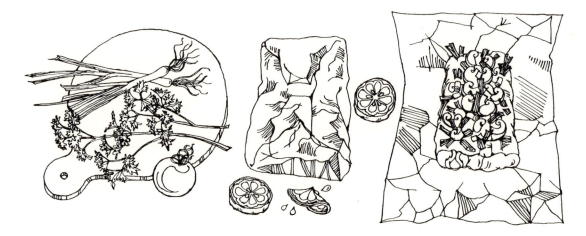

Plaice with Mustard Dressing

Cooking time: 12 minutes
Dish: oval platter.
Serves: 2

Calories per portion: 300

7½ oz. fresh or frozen plaice fillets
2 oz. butter *or* margarine
1 level teaspoon dry mustard

few drops of Worcestershire sauce
salt and black pepper

Place the fish in a grill pan, skin-side uppermost. Spread with 1 oz. of butter or margarine. Grill for 5 minutes. Meanwhile, cream the rest of the fat with the remaining ingredients. Turn the fish over, spread this mixture over the fish. Grill for a further 7 minutes, until cooked and golden brown.

Handy hint: make sure the mustard dressing is soft, so that it doesn't tear the flesh. Serve with a colourful salad.

Plaice Fillets in Sour Cream

Cooking time: 15 minutes
Time to stand
Oven: gas mark 5, 375°F
Dish: ovenproof dish (cooking)
individual dishes (serving)
Serves: 3–4

Calories per portion: 170–200

¼ pint single cream
2 teaspoons lemon juice
good pinch each of dill, thyme,
    mustard and ground ginger

salt and pepper
3–4 plaice fillets
½ oz. butter
paprika

Sour the cream by adding the lemon juice, and leave to stand for 30 minutes. Then add the herbs and seasonings. Skin plaice fillets, season and roll up. Melt butter in the dish, put in the rolled fillets, cover with foil and bake. When cooked, place fillets on a wire tray to cool. To serve, put fillets into individual dishes. Pour over a little of the sour cream sauce and garnish with paprika.

Handy hint: these look most attractive served on a bed of lettuce in real or glass scallop shells.

Hot Beefburger Savoury

Cooking time: 30 minutes
Pan: lidded frying pan
Dish: oval platter
Serves: 2

Calories per portion: 400

½ oz. butter
8 oz. frozen beefburgers with
    onion, cut into halves
1 medium onion, sliced
4 oz. white cabbage, shredded
4 oz. prepared sliced green beans

½ level teaspoon curry powder
salt and pepper to taste
1 tablespoon water
1 tomato, quartered *for garnish*

Melt the butter in a frying pan and fry beefburgers gently for 5 minutes, turning once. Remove from the pan and keep hot. Add the onion to pan and fry until transparent, then add the cabbage, beans, seasonings and water. Cover and simmer gently for 10–15 minutes over a low heat, adding beefburgers during the last few minutes of cooking. Pile on to a serving dish and garnish with tomato.

Handy hint: fry the beefburgers gently to retain their round shape.

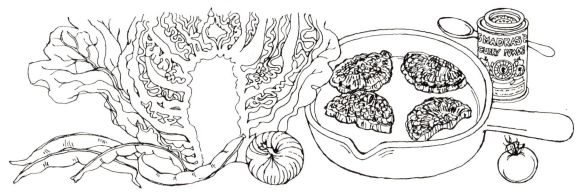

New Style Stew

Cooking time: 17 minutes
Dish: entrée dish
Serves: 4

Calories per portion: 300

1 oz. cooking fat
1 onion, sliced thinly
1 teaspoon flour
½ pint meat stock, *or* stock cube
    and water

11 oz. frozen steaklets
4 oz. frozen mixed vegetables
2 tomatoes, peeled and quartered
salt and pepper to taste

Melt the fat in a saucepan and fry the onion gently for 5 minutes. Stir in the flour. Add the stock gradually, stirring, then add the steaklets, mixed vegetables and tomatoes. Season, bring to boil, simmer for 12 minutes.

Handy hint: for those who are not slimming, serve with mashed potato.

Chinese Steaklets

Cooking time: 10 minutes
Dish: entrée dish
Serves: 4

Calories per portion: 220

½ oz. cooking fat
11 oz. frozen steaklets
1 leek, shredded finely
1 green pepper, cut into strips
2 oz. mushrooms, chopped

2 sticks celery, chopped finely
8 oz. can bean sprouts, drained
1 dessertspoon soy sauce
salt and pepper

Melt the fat in a frying pan and cook the steaklets as pack instructions. Remove steaklets and divide each one into three, crossways. Keep warm. Add the vegetables to the pan and fry for 5 minutes over a high heat, stirring all the time. Add the soy sauce and seasoning. Place the pieces of steaklets upright around a straight-sided dish and fill the circle with the vegetable mixture.

Handy hint: fry the steaklets gently to prevent curling.

Salad Medley

Cooking time: nil
Dish: oval platter
Serves: 4

Calories per portion: 420

2½ lb. cooked chicken
4 oranges, pith and peel removed, cut into segments
12 oz. tomatoes, skinned, de-seeded and cut into strips
3 medium heads of chicory, cut into pieces

2 tablespoons parsley, chopped
dressing
pinch each salt, pepper, dry mustard, sugar
4 tablespoons oil
2 tablespoons wine vinegar

Strip the meat from the chicken and cut into dice. Mix together with the orange, tomatoes, chicory and parsley. Put the seasonings in a basin, add the oil, then stir in the vinegar gradually. Add this dressing to the chicken mixture and pile on a platter.

Handy hint: to remove all skin and pith from the oranges, cut through the pith in a ½-inch wide spiral, using a serrated knife.

Oriental Chicken

Cooking time: 20 minutes
Dish: salad platter
Serves: 2

Calories per portion: 230

2 chicken joints
½ oz. butter
4 oz. prepared sliced green beans
4 oz. fresh bean shoots

soy sauce
salt and pepper
lettuce, and tomato *for garnish*

Remove the chicken meat from the bone and fry thoroughly in the butter; cool. Cook the sliced green beans but for only 2–3 minutes, drain and refresh under cold water. Blanch the bean shoots in boiling water for 15 seconds, drain and refresh. Mix the chicken, beans and bean shoots together with soy sauce and seasoning. Serve on a bed of lettuce, garnished with tomatoes.

Handy hint: if using frozen chicken, thaw overnight in the refrigerator, or place the unopened pack in cold water for about 1½ hours.

Chicken and Almonds

Cooking time: 30 minutes
Dish: oval platter
Serves: 4

Calories per portion: 300

4 chicken joints
2 oz. almonds, blanched, and cut into strips

1 oz. butter
watercress *for garnish*

Grill the chicken joints on each side for 10–15 minutes. Quickly fry the almonds in the butter until golden brown. Serve the chicken with the buttered almonds on top. Garnish with watercress.

Handy hint: blanch the almonds by pouring a small quantity of boiling water over them and allow to cool. The almonds can then be squeezed out of their papery skins.

Piquant Chicken

Cooking time: $\frac{3}{4}$–1 hour
Oven: gas mark 5, 375°F
Dish: ovenproof casserole
Serves: 4

Calories per portion: 170

4 chicken joints
1 large onion, sliced
15 oz. can tomatoes
3 teaspoons paprika

salt and pepper
5 oz. carton low fat natural yoghourt
watercress *for garnish*

Place the chicken joints, onion, tomatoes and seasonings in an ovenproof dish, mix well together. Cover and cook until the chicken is tender. Remove from the oven and pour the yoghourt over the chicken just before serving. Garnish with watercress.

Handy hint: for the non-slimming members of the family, serve with potatoes, baked in their jackets.

Cheese and Pea Salad

Cooking time: 8 minutes
Dish: salad platter or bowl
Serves: 3

Calories per portion: 300

8 oz. shelled peas (or frozen)
5 oz. processed cheese
1 spring onion

french dressing
2 tablespoons olive oil
1 tablespoon vinegar
pinch each of mustard, salt and sugar
lettuce leaves

Cook the peas for 8–10 minutes and leave until cold. Cut the cheese into $\frac{1}{4}$-inch cubes and chop the onion finely. Mix the peas, cheese and onion together, and just before serving, add dressing and toss. Serve surrounded by lettuce leaves.

Handy hint: alternatively, you can store some french dressing in a wide necked jar, and use in recipes as required.

Vegetable and Cream Salad

Cooking time: 8 minutes
Dish: oval platter
Serves: 3

Calories per portion: 170

8 oz. frozen mixed vegetables
4 inches cucumber, cubed
quarter bunch spring onions,
   trimmed and chopped

5 oz. carton soured cream
salt and pepper

Cook the mixed vegetables for 8 minutes. Cool. Mix together with the cucumber and chopped onion and fold in the soured cream. Season well and serve.

Handy hint: soured cream is not sour dairy cream. It is specially prepared commercially, and has a delicate tangy flavour.

Broccoli and Ham Rolls

Cooking time: 8 minutes
Dish: ovenproof entrée dish
Serves: 2
Colour picture, page 64

Calories per portion: 380

9 oz. frozen broccoli
4 slices of ham (4 oz.)

2 oz. cheese, grated
tomato wedges and watercress
   for garnish

Cook the broccoli for 10 minutes, drain. Place the spears on the slices of ham and roll up. Put in an ovenproof dish, sprinkle with cheese and grill until golden brown. Garnish with tomato and watercress.

Handy hint: make the grill very hot before placing the cheese-covered rolls under it. This prevents the cheese becoming oily.

Baked Mixed Vegetable Omelette

Cooking time: 15 minutes
Oven: gas mark 6, 400°F
Dish: round, shallow ovenproof
Serves: 2

Calories per portion: 320

4 oz. frozen mixed vegetables
$\frac{1}{4}$ oz. butter
3 eggs

2 oz. cheese, grated
1 tablespoon parsley, chopped
salt and pepper

Cook the mixed vegetables for 8 minutes, drain. Melt the butter in an oven-proof dish for a few minutes. Beat the eggs, add the cheese, mixed vegetables, parsley and seasoning. Pour into the prepared dish and bake. Serve immediately.

Handy hint: for non-slimmers add diced, cooked potato.

Grapefruit Sorbet

Cooking time: nil
Time to freeze
Dish: individual sundae glasses
or grapefruit skins
Serves: 4

Calories per portion: 70

$\frac{1}{4}$ oz. gelatine
artificial sweetener (if desired)
$\frac{1}{2}$ pint water

$6\frac{1}{4}$ fl. oz. can frozen concentrated
   grapefruit juice, thawed
1 egg white, whisked

Dissolve gelatine and sweetener in the water and add to the grapefruit juice. Stir well, pour mixture into ice tray and freeze for about one hour. Place mixture in a mixing bowl and fold in the egg white. Refreeze sorbet for at least two hours before serving.

Handy hint: if preferred, pour sorbet in used grapefruit skins and refreeze before serving.

Orange Jelly

Cooking time: nil
Mould: 1 pint
Serves: 4–5

Calories per portion: 110–150

3 oz. sugar
water
½ oz. gelatine

6¼ fl. oz. can frozen concentrated
    orange juice, thawed
juice of half lemon

Heat the sugar gently in a ¼ pint of water with the gelatine, stirring well until dissolved, and allow to cool. Pour the orange juice into a measure and make up to one pint with cold water, add the lemon juice, then stir in the gelatine mixture. Pour into a pint mould and allow to set.

Handy hint: to remove the jelly, immerse almost to top of mould in a bowl of hot water for a few seconds. Then place a plate over the mould and invert.

Raspberry Frou-frou

Cooking time: nil
Dish: individual sundae glasses
Serves: 3

Calories per portion: 70

8 oz. raspberries, fresh or frozen
artificial sweetener to taste
2 level teaspoons gelatine

2 tablespoons water
1 teaspoon lemon juice
1 egg white, whisked until stiff

Sprinkle the raspberries with sweetener and leave. Dissolve gelatine in the water, cool slightly then add to the lemon juice. Whisk until thick, fluffy and almost setting. Fold egg white and raspberries into the setting mixture and pile into individual glasses.

Handy hint: the gelatine will become 'ropy' if you boil the water in which it is dissolving. A metal spoon will show up the undissolved crystals better than a wooden one.

Orange Cheesecake

Cooking time: nil
Time to set
Tin: 6-inch cake tin
Dish: 8–9-inch platter
Serves: 8

Calories per portion: 120

8 oz. low fat curd cheese
5 oz. carton low fat natural
    yoghourt
½ oz. gelatine dissolved in 4
    tablespoons water

6¼ fl. oz. can frozen concentrated
    orange juice, thawed
artificial sweetener (if desired)
2 egg whites, whisked until stiff
1 orange *to decorate*

Line a loose-bottomed 6-inch cake tin with buttered greaseproof paper. Put curd cheese in a large bowl and combine with the yoghourt, dissolved gelatine and orange juice. Add sweetener, if desired, and fold in egg whites. Turn into prepared tin and leave to set in refrigerator. When set, turn out and decorate with orange segments.

Handy hint: to turn out, place the platter over the tin and invert. Press the loose bottom of the tin gently but firmly until the cheesecake slides out.

Index

USEFUL EQUIVALENT MEASURES

IMPERIAL	AMERICAN
1 teaspoon (3 teaspoons = 1 tablespoon)	1 teaspoon
1 tablespoon	1 tablespoon
1½ tablespoons	2 tablespoons
2 tablespoons	3 tablespoons
3 tablespoons	scant ¼ cup
4 tablespoons	5 tablespoons (⅓ cup)
5 tablespoons	6 tablespoons
5½ tablespoons	7 tablespoons
6 tablespoons (scant ¼ pint)	½ cup
¼ pint	⅔ cup
scant ½ pint	1 cup = 8 fluid ounces ½ pint (16 tablespoons)
½ pint (10 fluid ounces)	1¼ cups
generous ¾ pint (16 fluid ounces)	2 cups (1 pint)
1 pint (20 fluid ounces)	2½ cups

IMPERIAL	AMERICAN
flour—plain or self-raising	**flour—all-purpose**
½ ounce	2 tablespoons
1 ounce	¼ cup
4 ounces	1 cup
cornflour	**cornstarch**
1 ounce	¼ cup
generous 2 ounces	½ cup
4½ ounces	1 cup
sugar—castor or granulated	**sugar—granulated**
1 ounce	2 tablespoons
4 ounces	½ cup
7½ ounces	1 cup
sugar—soft brown, demerara	**sugar—light and dark brown**
1 ounce	2 tablespoons, firmly packed
8 ounces	1 cup, firmly packed
sifted icing sugar	**sifted confectioners' sugar**
1 ounce	¼ cup
4½ ounces	1 cup
butter, margarine, lard, dripping	**butter, margarine, shortening, drippings**
1 ounce	2 tablespoons
8 ounces	1 cup
grated cheese—Cheddar type Parmesan	**grated cheese—Cheddar type, Parmesan**
1 ounce	¼ cup
4 ounces	1 cup
vegetables and fruit	**vegetables and fruit**
2 ounces chopped pickled beet (root)	⅓ cup
7½ ounces chopped cooked spinach	1 cup
3—4 ounces button mushrooms	1 cup
4 ounces shelled peas	¾ cup
2 ounces bean sprouts	1 cup
4 ounces black/redcurrants, bilberries	1 cup
5 ounces raspberries	1 cup
5 ounces whole strawberries	1 cup
4 ounces smooth mashed potato	½ cup

IMPERIAL	AMERICAN
preserves	**preserves**
12 ounces clear honey, golden syrup, molasses, black treacle	1 cup (1 lb = 1⅓ cups)
11 ounces corn, maple syrup	1 cup
5—6 ounces jam, jelly, marmalade	½ cup
3 oz. chopped preserved ginger	⅓ cup
dried fruits and nuts	**dried fruits and nuts**
5—6 ounces raisins, currants, sultanas, chopped candied peel	1 cup
8 ounces stoned dates	1¼ cups pitted dates
8 ounces glacé cherries	1 cup candied cherries
6 ounces prunes (unsoaked)	1 cup
5—6 ounces dried apricots	1 cup
4 ounces halved shelled walnuts	1 cup
3—4 ounces pine nuts	1 cup
5 ounces whole shelled almonds	1 cup
4 ounces blanched slivered almonds	1 cup
7 ounces whole shelled peanuts	1 cup
4 ounces chopped nuts (most kinds)	1 cup
4 ounces ground almonds	1 cup
3 ounces desiccated coconut	1 cup shredded coconut
miscellaneous	**miscellaneous**
2 ounces soft bread/cake crumbs	1 cup
4 ounces fine dried bread-crumbs	1 cup
2 ounces cracker crumbs	¾ cup
7 ounces raw long grain rice (= 3½ cups cooked rice)	1 cup
3½ ounces rolled oats	.1 cup
6 ounces oatmeal	1 cup
1 ounce cornflakes	1 cup
1 ounce crushed cornflakes	⅔ cup
8 ounces minced raw meat	1 cup, firmly packed
8 ounces cottage cheese	1 cup
¼ pint single/double cream (5 fluid ounces)	½ cup plus 2 tablespoons (⅔ cup)
2 ounces curry powder	½ cup
5—6 ounces stoned olives	1 cup
2¾ ounces (smallest can) tomato purée	¼ cup tomato paste
¼ ounce gelatine	1 envelope gelatin
6 ounces peeled prawns	1 cup
6 ounces semi-sweet chocolate pieces	1 cup
1 ounce cooking chocolate	1 square